Great Trials in American History

About the Authors

Lee Arbetman An attorney and former elementary, junior high, and high school teacher, Arbetman has taught courses at Catholic University and at American University in their colleges of education. He is coauthor of *Street Law: A Course in Practical Law* (1980), as well as many articles about law-related education.

Richard L. Roe A graduate of Yale University and the University of Maine School of Law, Roe is Assistant Professor of Law at Georgetown University Law Center where he directs programs in which law students teach in high schools and correctional facilities.

Contributing Editor

Richard J. Morey Morey earned an M.A. in American history at the University of Delaware. He chairs the social studies department at the Prairie School in Racine, Wisconsin, where he teaches American, constitutional, and world history.

From The National Institute for Citizen Education in the Law and West Publishing Company

Great Trials in American History

Civil War to the Present

Lee Arbetman, M.Ed., J.D.
Adjunct Professor of Law
Georgetown University Law Center

Richard L. Roe, J.D.
Assistant Professor of Law
Georgetown University Law Center

Original text of the trials by Andrew David

West Publishing Company
St. Paul • New York • Los Angeles • San Francisco

Illustration credits: *American Law Register* 16; Chicago Historical Society 12; Defense Audio Visual Agency 163; *Dictionary of American Portraits* 28, 120; Reprinted with permission of *Esquire*. Copyright 1976 by Esquire Associates 121; *Harper's Weekly*/Library of Congress 18; *Harper's Weekly*/James L. Shaffer 3; Indiana Historical Society 8; Indiana State Library 5; Library of Congress 33, 57, 68, 91, 135, 187; John F. Marszalek, Jr. 14; Cynthia Meyer 95; National Archives 15, 42, 44, 53, 63; New York Historical Society 2; James L. Shaffer 98, 113, 129, 139, 143; Donald Tamaki 69; UPI/Bettmann Archives 30, 49, 51, 55, 65, 66, 75, 80, 88, 93, 115, 124, 128, 147, 153, 159; U.S. Air Force 38; U.S. Customs 103; U.S. Navy 41; Wide World Photos 26, 73, 82, 86, 102, 111, 137, 149, 165, 169, 172, 182; Copyright *Washington Post*. Reprinted by permission of the D.C. Public Library 190.

PICTURE RESEARCH assisted with the photo research.

Cover art: *The Heart of the Matter* by Sally Storch. Copyright © 1983 The West Collection, West Publishing Company.

GREAT TRIALS IN AMERICAN HISTORY is an adaptation of a four-volume series written by Andrew David and published by Lerner Publications. The original titles in the series were
  FAMOUS CRIMINAL TRIALS, 1979
  FAMOUS MILITARY TRIALS, 1980
  FAMOUS POLITICAL TRIALS, 1980
  FAMOUS SUPREME COURT CASES, 1980

COPYRIGHT © 1985 By WEST PUBLISHING CO.
          50 West Kellogg Boulevard
          P.O. Box 64526
          St. Paul, Minnesota 55164-9979

Library of Congress Cataloging in Publication Data

Arbetman, Lee.
  Great trials in American history.

  Includes index.
  1. Trials—United States.   I. Roe, Richard L.
II. Title.
KF220.A7   1984   345.73'02   84-5214
ISBN 0-314-80461-7   347.3052

Acknowledgments

We owe a considerable debt to Andrew David, the author of the original four-volume series from which *Great Trials in American History* was adapted. His extremely readable and engaging treatment of famous trials gave us the idea—and a substantial portion of the text—for this project.

Like other publications of the Institute, this one has in many ways been a group effort. We appreciate the support and guidance provided by our colleagues Charlotte Collins, Mary Curd-Larkin, Edward McMahon, Vivian Mills, Jason Newman, and Ed O'Brien. In addition we are grateful for the research assistance provided by Deborah Cotton, Diana Green, John Hicks, Jessica Holmes, Bruce James, Kenneth McGhee, Charlotte Melanson, Nancy Switkes, and Chris Welsh. Contributing editor Rick Morey has been unfailingly pleasant and patient in helping us tie the trials to the themes from the American experience that are taught in secondary school history classes. The completion of this project would have been impossible without the good cheer and capable work of our support staff: Linda Jones, Cathy Holloman, Linda Hilliard, Maria Hopkins, and Joyclyn Lyons. They keep the ship afloat.

A portion of this project was financially assisted under a series of grants from the Office of Juvenile Justice and Delinquency Prevention of the United States Department of Justice. Their support has been vital to the strengthening of law-related programs throughout the nation.

We are flattered that Louis Nizer, one of America's great trial lawyers and writers, has contributed a special foreward to this book. During his remarkable career, he has both tried and written about many of the greatest trials in American history. We hope this modest effort merits his approval.

LEE ARBETMAN
RICHARD L. ROE
WASHINGTON, D.C.
NOVEMBER, 1984

Advisory Committee of the National Institute for Citizen Education in the Law

The National Institute for Citizen Education in the Law

The National Institute for Citizen Education in the Law is an outgrowth of a Georgetown University program started in 1971 in which law students teach law courses in District of Columbia high schools, in juvenile and adult correctional institutions, and in a number of community based programs.

The Institute was created to promote increased opportunities for citizen education in law and is involved in course development, teacher training, and program replication. Other activities of the Institute include the provision of technical assistance and curriculum materials to law schools, school systems, departments of corrections, juvenile justice agencies, bar associations, legal service organizations, community groups, state and local governmental units, and others interested in establishing law-education programs.

The Institute is under the direction of a National Advisory Committee comprised of prominent individuals from the fields of law, education and public affairs. The Institute staff includes individuals with experience in both law and education.

For further information on Institute programs or materials contact it at 605 G Street N.W., Suite 401, Washington, D.C. 20001. Phone: (202) 624–8217.

Staff of the National Institute for Citizen Education in the Law

Director: Jason Newman
Co-Director: Edward O'Brien
Deputy Director—Legal Education: Edward McMahon
Deputy Director—Schools and Juvenile Justice: Lee Arbetman
Program Director—Juvenile Justice: Mary Curd-Larkin
Program Director—D.C. Schools and Corrections: Richard Roe
Program Director—Development & Management: Vivian Mills
Assistant Director—D.C. Schools: Robert L. Hayman, Jr.
Assistant Director—Budget Administration: Jeff Wilson
Support Staff: Linda D. Jones, Cathy Holloman, Linda Hilliard, Maria Hopkins, Joyclyn C. Lyons

Other Publications of The Institute And West Publishing Company

Street Law: A Course in Practical Law (1980)
Practical Law for Correctional Personnel (1981)
Law and the Consumer (1982)
Consumer Law: Competencies in Law and Citizenship (1982)
Family Law: Competencies in Law and Citizenship (1983)

Contents

Foreword

Disputes used to be settled by duels on the field of honor. Even in our country, Alexander Hamilton died in such a pistol duel. There came a time when trial by jury was used to decide who was right. The jury represents the public conscience. It exercises the judgment of the "common man." It evaluates a witness's truthfulness by observation and experience. It adds to its five senses two others—horse and common.

However, only the judge can instruct the members of the jury as to the rules of law by which they are bound. If the judge makes a mistake in stating the law, an appellate court will correct it. But the jury's finding of *facts* is rarely overruled because the appellate court has not seen or heard the witnesses. It only has a typewritten script of their testimony. It does not have the advantage of personal, intimate evaluation of the witness as he or she sits on the witness stand.

All this requires that each contestant be represented by a lawyer. In this way, what is called the "adversary system" is achieved. A legal philosopher put it this way: "Each lawyer shows his clients's best profile. The judge and jury see truth full face."

The lawyer is the civilized fighter for truth. Cross-examination is a scalpel to excise lies from a witness's mind. No better method has yet been found to do so.

Our legal rules, especially in criminal cases, result from a fear of governmental tyranny. In ancient times, it was the king's tyranny. But we still fear the government's power against the lone individual. The federal government has the FBI and prosecutors. The state governments have district attorneys and a flood of detectives and police officers. That is why our Constitution has deliberately thrown a cordon of protective devices around the defendant in a criminal case. The Fifth Amendment protects defendants from being compelled to testify against themselves—a technique once used by tyrants to convict defendants, no matter what they did.

In our criminal justice system, the burden is on the prosecutor to prove a defendant guilty. More than this, the jury must be convinced of the defendant's guilt beyond a reasonable doubt. This is a severe standard. But before we deprive a citizen of his or her liberty, our Constitution places these obstacles in the path of the all powerful government forces. No doubt this makes it possible for some guilty defendants to go free. But as the Supreme Court has said, "This is the price we pay for a civilized society."

Decisions in the courts do not merely determine the rights between two litigants. They establish principles that guide our society. Thus, significant decisions become landmarks bearing the names of the individuals who litigated the issues. The trials in this book are each, in their special way, landmark cases. For instance, the Supreme Court decided in the *Scottsboro* trials that a state must provide effective assistance of a lawyer for persons charged with serious crimes. The *Escobedo* and *Miranda* cases further defined the right to counsel; police now routinely inform persons whom they arrest of their rights to be silent and to have counsel. In the *Gault* case, the right to counsel was extended to juveniles.

I have been pleased to represent clients whose cases have also established significant legal principles on important issues. The *John Henry Faulk* case established the principle that blacklists against television performers who were suspected of being "fellow travelers" (that is, Communists) were illegal. This was the only case in my career in which the jury awarded more punitive damages than I requested. Another historic case was the libel suit of a famous war correspondent, Quentin Reynolds, against a columnist, Westbrook Pegler. The large amount of money awarded by the jury, including punitive damages, put a brake upon the excesses of the media without compromising the right of free speech. It established a balance between an individual's rights and the public policy of free speech. If the scales tip too heavily on one side, the First Amendment right may get a bad name for extremism. If they tip on the other side, it interferes with the precious fundamental right of free speech. The importance of the *Reynolds-Pegler* and *Faulk* cases was demonstrated by the fact that one of them was made into a Broadway play, *A Case of Libel,* and later a television special, and the *Faulk* case was portrayed in a prime-time program entitled "Fear on Trial" on national television.

The health of our political system depends mainly on the condition of our judicial system. As John Marshall, the first chief justice of the United States, said: "Constitutional government is only as good as the courts; no better, no worse. The laws are promises. They are kept or broken in the courts."

The judicial system is a human structure and therefore is not perfect. Continuous criticisms of it are justified in many instances. This should not blind us to the fact that the American judicial system is as good if not better than any other in the world. I set forth the following reasonable approach to evaluate it:

Perfect justice—impossible.
Approximate justice—acceptable.
Efforts to improve the quality of justice—always!

The students and teachers who use this book will come away with a greater awareness of the protective, positive aspects of the law. A young person's respect for the law will foster his or her respect for individual freedoms and for the democratic process. As an author of books intended to explain the intricacies of the legal process to the layperson, I applaud the noble purposes of *Great Trials in American History.* Young people who read this text will be better citizens.

LOUIS NIZER
NEW YORK CITY
OCTOBER 1984

Introduction

Before going on a trip in the family car, it is a good idea to trace your route on a highway map. That way, you will have a picture in your mind of the most important features of the trip: the distance you will cover, the kinds of highways you will be traveling on, the places along the way where you might stop, and the major roads that will cross your path.

This introduction offers you a kind of highway map for this book. It marks out for you the important features that you will encounter along the way as you read about what happened in the great trials. Because it gives you an overview of what to watch for, this introduction can help make your progress through each legal case smoother and more rewarding.

LAW AND HISTORY

Our system of law has significantly affected the course of American history. By the same token, historical forces have affected the way laws have been written, interpreted, and enforced. Law and history are so closely interwoven that it is impossible to separate one from the other.

Every law we have reflects in some way a value or set of values that we hold as a people. We have laws requiring children to attend school until a certain age because we place great value on the importance of being educated. If there were no such laws, many people would be unable to read and write, would have a hard time getting and keeping a job, and would be at a disadvantage in taking part in important citizenship activities like voting, holding public office, or serving on a jury.

Values sometimes change. Sometimes, it is only a matter of a shift in emphasis, but now and then a significant change occurs. For example, in colonial America slavery was legal. Today it is not. The very idea of keeping any one person or a whole group of persons in bondage became unacceptable. Laws that at one time permitted slavery were repealed. New laws were passed prohibiting slavery.

Values can also come into conflict with each other from time to time. Most Americans, for example, value both a free press and fair trials for defendants in criminal cases. But is it possible for a defendant's attorney to choose impartial jurors when the press has reported widely about a particularly sensational crime? This is one of many instances in which two positive values collide.

In the great trials recounted in this book, basic values were almost always at issue. The courtroom became an arena in which the participants fought over legal issues closely connected to important social values. Through the process of resolving such value conflicts, much of America's history has been written.

YOU AS THE STUDENT OF HISTORY

Like your counterparts in schools throughout the country, you are required to study American history. This requirement—a kind of "mini-law"—rests on an important value, just as actual laws do. In this case, the value being expressed is society's belief in the importance of education that equips members of society to function as informed citizens. In a democratic society like ours, where power resides with the people, citizens need a clear picture of the nation's beginning, its ideals, and its development. In order to make intelligent decisions in the present, we need to know about the past.

In reading *Great Trials*, you will learn about the role that law has played in the life of our nation. This experience will not only enrich your understanding of American history but will also sharpen your skills as a citizen. As you go through each trial, you will learn about the content of the law involved and also about the way our legal system works. As you are reading, you may find it useful to ask yourself questions like these:

- Could I have solved the problem in the case without using the legal system? If so, how?
- Do the procedures that were used square with my own sense of fair play?
- If I had been on the jury (or had been the judge), how would I have decided this case?

- Did this trial settle the issue once and for all?
  Or is it still with us today?
- How does this issue affect my life?

DIFFERENT TYPES OF LEGAL PROCEEDINGS

In choosing the title for this book, we used "trials" in a broad sense to cover a variety of formal legal proceedings held to determine guilt or innocence or to settle disputes. Only a few of the fifteen proceedings included here represent actual courtroom trials. Others involve appeals. Still others involve various types of military trials called courts-martial.

Probably the best-known legal proceeding, thanks in part to television and movies, is the courtroom trial. In a trial, two or more persons who are in conflict present evidence and arguments before a "trier of fact"—a judge or a jury. One or more lawyers represent each side and question the witnesses. The judge rules on legal questions that come up during the trial and also sees to it that both sides observe the rules and procedures. Then the jury (or the judge, if there is no jury) decides the outcome of the case.

A party that loses in a trial often has the right to appeal to a higher court. An appeal is a legal proceeding in which one party seeks to change the decision of the trial court. At an appeals hearing, each side presents arguments on specific legal issues in dispute to a panel of judges (instead of just one judge). There are no witnesses or jurors. The rules do not permit new evidence to be presented. The appeals court can uphold or reverse the decision of the trial court.

A court-martial is a special kind of trial that involves military law, and it takes place in a military setting with military personnel as the participants. Although it is similar to a civilian trial, a court-martial uses special procedures set forth in the Uniform Code of Military Justice. Sometimes a court-martial is preceded by a court of inquiry. The court of inquiry does not decide whether the accused is guilty but rather whether there is enough information to convene a court-martial. Military law also has a process of appeal. Once a verdict is reached, it can be appealed to the commanding officers in whose jurisdiction the court-martial was held. Beyond that it may be possible to appeal to a military court of review in Washington, D.C., and finally to the Court of Military Appeals.

The important point to keep in mind is that all these proceedings—despite their differences—serve a common purpose: determining which side in a dispute should prevail by applying accepted legal principles to factual situations.

DIFFERENCES BETWEEN CRIMINAL AND CIVIL TRIALS

In our legal system, we distinguish between criminal and civil law. The rules of procedure differ for each, and different standards are used for deciding the outcome. This book includes both categories of trials, so you will want to be familiar with the differences.

In a criminal case, the government takes action against (prosecutes) a party (the defendant) accused of committing a crime. To find the defendant guilty, the judge or jury must be convinced of guilt beyond a reasonable doubt.

In a civil case, one or more private parties (plaintiffs) take action against (sue) another party or parties (defendants) for some breach of duty or breach of agreement. For the plaintiff to win, the court must believe that the preponderance (i.e., majority) of the evidence is on his or her side.

THE ROLE OF THE COURTS

Our Constitution—the basic law of the land—proclaims certain principles that form the underpinnings of our open, democratic society. These principles are spelled out for the most part in the Bill of Rights, which is made up of the first ten amendments to the Constitution. In the great trials chronicled in this book, three of these principles clearly emerge: *liberty, equality,* and *justice.*

Important principles like liberty, equality, and justice represent ideals toward which we, as a people, strive. They are so important, in fact, that the Constitution assigns the job of interpreting and protecting them to one branch of government—the judicial branch—which includes all the courts. The ultimate protector of these principles is the highest court in the land, the Supreme Court, whose rulings often go to the heart of constitutional law.

By giving the courts the primary responsibility for protecting these principles, the drafters of the Constitution and the Bill of Rights were saying, in effect, that such matters as liberty, equality, and justice should not be subject to popular vote. Fundamental issues of law should be weighed and decided in an atmosphere that encourages careful study and deliberation, away from the shifting moods of the public. Thus, throughout the federal court system and in many state courts as well, judges are not elected to office but instead are appointed. This is one device that removes them from the rough-and-tumble of everyday political pressures. It also reduces the possibility that a judge will get into office only on the basis of his or her stand on a popular issue. Equally important, it protects judges from being removed from office just for having made unpopular rulings.

Because the judicial branch is separated from the rest of government and the political system, it might be easy to imagine that judges deal only with dry, technical, or abstract doctrines. On the contrary, as you become involved in these great trials, you will notice that courts enter into the thick of everyday human issues. More than that, sometimes they boldly assert public policy and in so doing stir up significant controversy.

Keep in mind, however, that the ideals of liberty, equality, and justice are not simply words carved in stone. They are dynamic forces in the life of the nation. When a court finds that a citizen has been denied the equal protection of the law that is his or her right, or that a basic liberty such as freedom of speech is being restricted, or that any kind of injustice is being tolerated, the court should say so, clearly and emphatically. Our success in achieving the ideals of liberty, equality, and justice is some measure of how well the nation is meeting the challenge of constitutional democracy.

LIBERTY

The accounts in this book that deal with liberty concern the basic freedoms found in the First Amendment of the Bill of Rights—the freedoms of speech, press, religion, petition, and assembly. Although these freedoms lie at the very heart of a democratic society, they are not absolute. Sometimes they come into conflict with other very important rights. When this has happened, the courts have often been looked to for help.

During the years following World War I, General William "Billy" Mitchell argued that the United States should strengthen its young air forces and give much greater emphasis to the role of air power in military planning. This was not the official position of the military, but Mitchell spoke out anyway. The First Amendment usually protects citizens' rights to express themselves peacefully on matters of public importance. In this instance, however, Mitchell's First Amendment rights came into direct conflict with the need to follow the orders of superiors in the military command. Eventually, Mitchell was court-martialed, found guilty of making statements that were detrimental to military discipline, and suspended from the Army for five years. Years later his views about the importance of air power were proved correct by the events of history. The case of General Billy Mitchell, along with several others in *Great Trials*, illustrates how First Amendment liberties, though not absolute, help preserve our free society.

EQUALITY

The Fourteenth Amendment's guarantee of "equal protection of the laws" is the constitutional cornerstone of the concept of equality. The basic freedoms in the Bill of Rights cannot be provided to only some of the people. Under our laws, unequal treatment may constitute illegal discrimination that violates the ideal of equality. Some cases involving the issue of equality are not at all clear-cut, however.

In the chapter about Allan Bakke, we learn that a white engineer was denied admission to medical school because a certain number of places had been reserved by the university for minority applicants. Bakke had higher grades and test scores than some of the minority applicants. Admission to highly competitive professional schools is usually based on past performance in school. Rewarding people based on individual achievement seems to be sensible public policy. On the other hand, decades of discrimination have limited opportunities for blacks, Hispanics, and other minorities to enter the medical profession. Graduating more minority doctors also seems to be a legitimate policy for the university to pursue. The *Bakke* case raises a number of complex questions about equality: can some people be treated more favorably without discriminating against others? Can programs be designed to make up for past discrimination without punishing individuals who were not responsible for that discrimination? *Bakke* and several other cases in this book demonstrate how Americans have used the legal system to pursue the elusive ideal of equality.

JUSTICE

Both the Fifth and the Fourteenth Amendments prohibit the government from depriving an individual of "life, liberty, or property without due process of law." The promise of due process is a major component of the American ideal of justice. Although philosophers and others have debated the meaning of justice, for our purposes justice can be thought of as fairness. The courts have looked at the idea of fairness in two ways: (1) is the law fair? and (2) are fair procedures used to enforce the law? These procedures are also established by laws in many cases.

The case of Gerald Gault provided the U.S. Supreme Court with an opportunity to consider a very important question about justice: what procedures should be used when juveniles are charged with a crime and brought into court? Although the courts and legal system generally treated offenders in the nineteenth century very harshly in the early part of the twentieth century all the states began to establish special juvenile courts. These juvenile courts adopted very informal procedures as they attempted to assist and rehabilitate juvenile delinquents instead of punishing them as adult criminals. However, some of the programs to help children still seemed like punishment, and the informal procedures also left them with few of the rights and protections available to adults in the criminal justice system. In *Gault,* the Supreme Court took a close look at the juvenile justice system in order to determine what procedures were required to satisfy contemporary notions of justice and due process.

THE ISSUE OF FEDERALISM

The fifteen cases in *Great Trials* illustrate how Americans have used the legal system in their search for liberty, equality, and justice. The challenge of such a search is made even greater in our federal system because power is shared between the national government and the state governments. Should fundamental legal values such as liberty, equality, and justice have one meaning throughout the entire country, or should individual states be able to determine what these values mean for the people within their borders?

This question of shared power comes up most frequently in cases occurring after 1950, when the U.S. Supreme Court increasingly applied the protections of the Bill of Rights to the states. Originally, the Bill of Rights protected citizens from violation of certain fundamental rights by the federal government. After the Civil War, however, the Fourteenth Amendment was passed as part of a series of amendments designed to assure full legal protections for the former slaves. The language of the Fourteenth Amendment prohibits the states from violating the "due process" and "equal protection" rights of all citizens. During the twentieth century, the Supreme Court began to interpret the word "due process" to mean all the fundamental rights from the Bill of Rights. Increasingly, the Court required the states to observe these rights. This change in interpretation came about slowly and with some difficulty. The courts had to balance the interests of the states in maintaining their sovereign powers against the interests of individual citizens in having their basic constitutional rights protected against possible violation by state government. Consequently the question of whether state or federal power should prevail in a specific legal question—the issue of federalism—remains an important ingredient in the search for constitutional ideals.

IMPROVING OUR SYSTEM OF JUSTICE

Americans are committed to making the justice system live up to its name. Taking the journey in this book along the legal pathway from the Civil War to the present, you will notice many positive changes in the way the justice system operates. The system is not perfect, however. Nor is it in its final form. *Great Trials* tries to present a balanced, realistic view of a system that has changed to reflect contemporary notions of fairness. In some of the cases in *Great Trials*, appellate courts corrected injustices and established important precedents that brought us closer to the ideals of liberty, equality, and justice. Other cases may leave us wondering whether justice has really been done. As citizens, we have a responsibility to learn about and participate in the justice system in order to improve it.

The cases in *Great Trials* are not necessarily famous because of the specific acts of the persons involved. The greatness of these cases rests instead with the significance of the legal issues raised at trial and on appeal. The decisions made in these cases and the public's reactions to them have had an impact on our history; the public clamor that many of them aroused have also been a reflection of our history. Many of the legal issues, even from the older cases, remain perplexing dilemmas that are still debated today. Your study of *Great Trials* will enable you to understand and contribute to the discussion of some of the most important issues of our time.

Great Trials in American History

1

"Major General" Lambdin P. Milligan

BACKGROUND

During the Civil War, many Americans felt threatened and endangered even though they lived far from the actual battlefields. For citizens in some seemingly peaceful areas, the war was closer than a modern observer might imagine.

Such an area was Huntington, Indiana. It was well north of the border between the North and South where much of the fighting had taken place. But this town, like others in the Midwest, contained a number of Confederate sympathizers known as Copperheads. Some northerners considered the Copperheads no more than cranks or nuisances, but others, including President Lincoln, saw them as a genuine threat to the cause of Union victory.

By 1864, many people in the Union were anxious to see the Civil War ended after three and a half years of strife. The previous year had seen a week of antidraft riots in New York City. President Lincoln's leadership had been attacked by members of his own cabinet as well as political opponents.

Lincoln had previously organized the Union into military districts, headed by military commanders. These commanders helped recruit soldiers and gather local resources for the war. They also arrested citizens believed to be dangerous to the Union.

Lambdin P. Milligan, an alleged Copperhead, was arrested, tried, and convicted in a military court assembled near the town of Huntington. The court-martial found Milligan, a civilian, guilty of treason. He was sentenced to be hanged. In the court-martial, Milligan did not have the same rights as in civilian court. He did not get a trial by jury, for example.

1

Angry New Yorkers riot against the Union draft policy that allowed wealthy men to hire substitutes to take their places in the army in the Civil War.

Milligan's lawyers asked the federal court in Indiana to release Milligan. They argued that the military did not have the legal power to convict and sentence a civilian in Milligan's situation.

Milligan's case reached the Supreme Court after the Civil War had ended. It raised the important question of whether the military forces could legally try civilians during wartime. Many Americans believed that some liberties of the individual must give way to a broader concern for national security in time of war. Others were concerned that if a civilian could be tried by the military when normal civilian courts were operating, the military could become more powerful than the democratically elected government.

THE MILLIGAN CASE

On a bright autumn day in October 1864, a train backed slowly down the tracks of the Wabash railroad in Huntington, Indiana, about ninety miles northeast of Indianapolis. As it approached a house near the railroad tracks, the train came slowly to a stop. A squadron of soldiers, dressed in the dark blue uniforms of the Union Army, hurried out of one of the railroad cars and headed directly for the house, their rifles at the ready.

Inside the house was a tall, broad-shouldered man named Lambdin P. Milligan. Formerly, Milligan had been a teacher, but he was now a lawyer active in local politics. Although he looked strong and healthy, he was actually a very sick man. And he was not feeling at all well on that autumn day when the Union soldiers rushed into his house and put him under arrest.

At the time Milligan was arrested, the American Civil War had been going on for more than three years. The war had already taken more American lives than any previous war in American history.

THE COPPERHEAD PARTY.——IN FAVOR OF *A VIGOROUS PROSECUTION OF PEACE!*

An 1863 cartoon pictured the Copperheads as snakes who would strike without warning.

3

During the Civil War, Indiana was allied with the North, but the sympathies of many of the state's citizens were on the side of the South. In Indiana and other northern states, there were secret societies composed of people called **Copperheads,** who were enthusiastic supporters of the Confederate cause. The Copperheads aided the South by spying, by encouraging and even helping Union soldiers to desert the Union Army, by propaganda campaigns, by sabotage, and by other terror tactics.

THE SONS OF LIBERTY

In July 1864, several months before the raid on Lambdin Milligan's house, a group of civilians had gathered outside a Union Army camp near Indianapolis. They were frightened, and they demanded to see the officer in charge, Brigadier General Henry Carrington. The civilians claimed that various members of a Copperhead organization called the Sons of Liberty had approached them and demanded that they join the secret group and work for the South. The Copperheads had threatened to harm them if they did not cooperate, and these citizens wanted protection. When General Carrington agreed to help them, they revealed that the Sons of Liberty were also planning to seize the government arsenal in Indianapolis. If they succeeded, and if they received military assistance from the Confederacy, the Copperheads believed that they would then be able to capture the entire state of Indiana.

General Carrington asked who the members of this **radical** group were, and the people named some names, including that of "Major General" Lambdin P. Milligan. Milligan held the rank of "major general" in the Sons of Liberty, but he was not a real major general. In fact, he had no official rank, because he was not in the military forces of any established army. Milligan was a civilian, a Copperhead, and a member of the Sons of Liberty.

The attack on the Indianapolis arsenal never took place, although the Union forces were prepared for it. But General Carrington kept a record of what the civilians had told him, including the names of those who seemed to be involved.

During the rest of that spring and summer, things began going badly for the Confederate forces. By fall, the tide of battle had turned in favor of the Union. In October, a new officer named General Alvin Hovey took command of the Indiana military district. Hovey believed that the city of Indianapolis was filled with enemy officers and Southern sympathizers who were plotting **treason** and that the entire state was in danger. As part of his defense against this threat, Hovey sent a group of his soldiers to the house of Lambdin Milligan, where they arrested him and took him off to the Union Army camp prison.

TRIAL OR COURT-MARTIAL?

Milligan was charged with conspiracy to commit treason, giving aid to the enemy, and violating the laws of war. General Hovey appointed a **military commission** of officers from his own staff and brought Milligan to be tried by **court-martial** before them. But Milligan complained that the army had no right to try him under military law because he was a civilian. General Hovey ignored Milligan's argument and conducted the court-martial anyway. Milligan was put on trial with three other Copperheads, although his lawyers had tried unsuccessfully to have him tried separately.

When the trial got under way, the **judge advocate** who was prosecuting the four men described Milligan as "the right arm of this conspiracy in this state, the active, energetic and venomous leader. A man of unquestioned ability and determination, and with a heart full of hatred, envy and malice, he moved forward in this

The military commission that tried Lambdin Milligan.

scheme of revolution with a coolness and intensity of purpose, not exceeded by another member of the conspiracy."

Although the evidence against them was strong, all four men had pleaded "not guilty." Midway through the trial, however, one of the defendants decided to change his plea to "guilty," in return for an offer of **immunity** from the judge advocate. He agreed to testify against his associates in return for a promise that he would not be prosecuted further if he did so. This defendant then testified against the remaining three defendants. Milligan and the other two were found guilty, and they were sentenced to be hanged. The date for the hanging was set for May 19, 1865, six months in the future.

PRESIDENT LINCOLN'S INVOLVEMENT

At that point, Lambdin Milligan's lawyer went to Washington to plead his case directly before President Abraham Lincoln. He was received by the president but he was unsuccessful in his arguments on Milligan's behalf. President Lincoln upheld the authority of General Hovey to try Milligan under military law. The president did say, however, that if the war came to an end before the hanging took place, he might be able to **commute** Milligan's sentence and give him a prison term instead of executing him.

The Civil War ended in April 1865, but only five days later Abraham Lincoln was assassinated. Vice President Andrew Johnson became president, and he, of course, knew nothing of the private conversation that had taken place between Milligan's lawyer and President Lincoln.

THE FINAL APPEAL

Nine days before Milligan was scheduled to hang, his lawyer went before the **circuit court** of Indiana and asked for Milligan's release on the grounds that Milligan was being held in prison illegally. The circuit court judges could not reach a decision, and they referred the question to the U.S. Supreme Court, meanwhile postponing Milligan's execution. A month later, before the Supreme Court could consider the case, Milligan's sentence was commuted to life imprisonment by President Andrew Johnson.

While Johnson's act of mercy may have saved Milligan's life, it failed to answer two important questions. First, had Lambdin Milligan been legally imprisoned? Second, did the armed forces have the right to try a civilian under military law? These were questions that the Supreme Court would have to decide.

THE MERRYMAN CASE

This was not the first time that a case of this kind had been brought before the courts. In the early days of the Civil War, a young civilian named John Merryman was arrested by the Union Army for "acts disloyal to the United States government." Merryman was imprisoned in an army camp, and his lawyer went directly to the chief justice of the Supreme Court in Washington to plead his client's case.

Roger B. Taney, the chief justice at that time, not only served on the Supreme Court but also sat as a circuit court judge in Baltimore, Maryland. (In this period of the nation's history, Supreme Court justices were also responsible for particular circuit court districts in which they heard cases.) In his capacity as circuit court judge, Taney heard Merryman's case and then issued a **writ of habeas corpus,** a legal document demanding that Merryman be brought to court so that the legality of his imprisonment could be determined. When the Union general holding Merryman refused repeatedly to bring his prisoner to court, Taney charged him with contempt of court.

Acting as chief justice of the Supreme Court, Taney wrote an opinion on the Merryman case, which was presented to President Abraham Lincoln. The chief justice explained that the general who had imprisoned Merryman claimed he had been authorized by the president to ignore a writ of habeas corpus in times of war or civil strife. But this was not possible, Taney noted, because, according to the Constitution, the right of habeas corpus could only be suspended by an act of Congress, not by a presidential order.

President Lincoln gave no answer to the chief justice's opinion. Instead, he went directly to Congress and asked that a law be passed giving the president the authority to suspend the writ of habeas corpus in a wartime situation. Congress obliged him by immediately passing such a law. There was nothing more that the chief justice could do, and John Merryman remained in prison.

The years passed, the war came to an end, and John Merryman was released from prison. But now Lambdin Milligan's case was going before the Supreme Court for a ruling on a subject very similar to the one that had been argued five years earlier. The Milligan case was important. At issue was the question of what would happen to the American system of justice if the armed forces had the power to arrest, imprison, and try civilians while suspending some of their constitutional rights at the same time. Who had the ultimate authority over civilians in time of war, the armed forces or the civil courts?

THE SUPREME COURT ACTS IN THE MILLIGAN CASE

The case of Lambdin Milligan was officially brought before the Supreme Court on March 6, 1866. As lawyers on both sides of the issue presented their cases before the Court, Lambdin Milligan sat in a cell in a federal penitentiary in Ohio that he had become quite used to by now. The defense lawyers argued that Milligan had been denied a fair trial. The military had no right to imprison him nor to put him on trial; this should have been the responsibility of the civilian authorities. Because Milligan's trial had been illegal, they maintained, so were the findings and sentence of that trial.

The lawyers for the United States, on the other hand, argued that the trial had been completely legal. They pointed out that Congress had given the president the power to authorize the military to hold civilians in prison during wartime. This power, they argued, implied that the military could also try and sentence a civilian for such crimes as disloyalty or treason. A state of war, they concluded, often required certain adjustments to be made in our system of justice, and this was a definite case in point.

Lambdin P. Milligan

The Supreme Court considered Lambdin Milligan's case for three weeks before delivering its opinion. The main question of this case, the Court said, was: "Had this **[military] tribunal** the legal power and authority to try and punish this man? . . . The importance of the main question . . . cannot be overstated; for it involves the very framework of the government and the fundamental principles of American liberty." Since the courts in Indiana were open and operating when Milligan was brought before a military commission, "no usage of war could **sanction** a military trial there for any offense whatever of a citizen in civil life. . . . One of the plainest constitutional provisions was, therefore, infringed when Milligan was tried by a court not ordained and established by Congress, and not composed of judges. . . ." Finally, Milligan had been denied another of his constitutional rights, said the Court, when he was not allowed a **trial by jury.**

THE LIMITS OF MARTIAL LAW

But the Court made clear that its opinion did not decide the government's power to proclaim **martial law** in situations of war or civil unrest. In instances such as a civil war or in the event of a foreign invasion, martial law could be proclaimed when the courts and the civil authorities are unable to function effectively. But it also said that martial law "cannot arise from a threatened invasion. The necessity must be actual and present . . . such as effectually closes the courts and deposes the civil administration. . . . Martial rule can never exist where the courts are open. . . ."

The courts had indeed been "open" in Indiana when Lambdin Milligan was arrested and tried in 1864. At that time, Indiana was not a battleground, and martial law should not have been substituted for civil law. The Supreme Court concluded that the military commission that had tried Milligan had been illegally constituted. Therefore, his conviction and sentence should be reversed.

Lambdin Milligan was not released from prison because he had been innocent but because his trial had been illegal. Some people said that it was wrong to release a man who was accused of crimes as serious as treason. But a greater good had come from Milligan's case. From that day forward, the Supreme Court's ruling ensured that all citizens would be guaranteed their basic constitutional rights to a fair trial even in time of war or national emergency, as long as the civil authorities were functioning. The Court's decision

9

limited the powers of the military and upheld the rights of civilians and the greater authority of the civil laws that protect them in war as well as in peace.

Testing Your Understanding

1. Why was Lambdin P. Milligan considered a Copperhead?

2. With what crimes was Milligan charged?

3. When the case reached the Supreme Court in 1866, what did Milligan's lawyers argue? What were the government's arguments?

4. Why do you think a military rather than a civilian court took action against Milligan?

5. What was the Supreme Court's decision in this case? What reasons did it give?

6. Do you think that Milligan would have preferred a trial by a jury of his peers? Why or why not?

7. Given the strong evidence against Milligan, was it fair for the Supreme Court to order his release from prison? Give reasons for your answer.

2
Cadet
Johnson Whittaker

BACKGROUND

Following the Civil War, the legal status of millions of blacks was changed from "slave" to "citizen." The Thirteenth Amendment of the Constitution outlawed slavery. The Fourteenth and Fifteenth Amendments gave the former slaves full citizenship, including the right to vote. Under the Reconstruction program passed by Congress after the war, martial law was imposed throughout the South. Federal troops tried to enforce the new rights guaranteed to blacks.

For a few years after the Civil War, some people believed that blacks would be able to live side by side with whites on equal footing. But the attitudes and circumstances of several centuries of slavery were hard to overcome. Voting rights of blacks were limited by poll taxes and literacy tests. Schools for blacks were few and not well financed. Most blacks worked in the fields as sharecroppers, not much differently from when they were slaves.

In April of 1877, Reconstruction came to an official end when the last group of federal troops left the South. Later that year, President Rutherford B. Hayes told southern blacks their rights and interests would be safer if the federal government let the South alone. The words "let alone" signaled a retreat from the equality promised for blacks that had begun with the Civil War.

The U.S. Army itself was segregated and had been since the Revolution. During the Civil War, black troops fought in many major battles, but the black units were kept separate from white units and black units were almost always led by white officers. Black soldiers were denied equal pay and equal rank. After the Civil

11

Black soldiers served under white officers in the Union Army during the Civil War.

War, the army continued to be segregated and was not integrated until after World War II.

The U.S. Military Academy at West Point was not closed to young black men after the Civil War. But the few blacks who attended West Point were treated differently from whites by the other cadets. No blacks roomed with whites and white cadets rarely talked to or spent time with black cadets. It appeared as if the belief in racial inferiority of blacks—a belief that supported the system of segregation in the South—was also common at the military academy.

Johnson Whittaker, the son of a slave and a slave himself as a child, seemed to have the ability to become a good army officer. For two years before enrolling at West Point in 1876, he had been in college in South Carolina. But his years as a cadet were difficult ones. Despite the setback he suffered at West Point, his accomplishments in his adult years proved that he had the ability to succeed.

THE WHITTAKER CASE

The U.S. Military Academy at West Point is located on a picturesque bluff overlooking the Hudson River, about fifty miles north of New York City. It is here that young cadets receive a college education and are trained to be officers in the U.S. Army. Many famous generals in American history, including Ulysses S. Grant, Robert E. Lee, John J. Pershing, Dwight D. Eisenhower, and Douglas MacArthur, have graduated from West Point. West Point was founded in 1802, and over the many years of its existence, a number of school traditions have developed. Some of those traditions were not at all pleasant, as a young cadet named Johnson Whittaker found out.

FROM THE PLANTATION TO WEST POINT

Johnson Whittaker was born in 1858, the son of a slave mother who worked on a large plantation in Camden, South Carolina. As a young boy, Johnson Whittaker lived on the plantation, and he saw it partially destroyed by the Union Army in the final days of the Civil War. As time went on, however, he turned out to be more fortunate than most black children were in those days. He received a fairly good education and even began college in South Carolina. Then, at the age of eighteen, Whittaker was accepted as a cadet by the U.S. Military Academy. In 1876, he arrived at West Point full of fear, excitement, awe, and pride, eager to begin a new life that had opened up for him.

There was only one other black cadet, Henry Flipper, at West Point at that time, and when Whittaker arrived, they became roommates. After a year, Henry Flipper became the first black to graduate from West Point in the academy's history. Whittaker was left as the only black person at the school, and he was not assigned another roommate. Life was not easy for anyone at West Point, but for Whittaker it was especially difficult. One of the not-so-nice traditions at West Point was the "silent treatment." Because he was black, Whittaker was subjected to the "silent treatment," which meant that the white cadets would not socialize with him in any way and would speak to him only when they were required to for official reasons. As a result, Whittaker got no help or support from the other cadets in his studies, his military training, or his personal life.

Johnson Whittaker as a West Point cadet.

A STRANGE INCIDENT

Nevertheless, Johnson Whittaker managed to survive in this silent world for four years. But because he had been forced to repeat a year due to poor grades, Whittaker still had another year to complete at West Point. As his junior year was coming to a close, it looked as if he would pass into his senior year. But something changed all that. One morning in April 1880, Johnson Whittaker was discovered unconscious in his room, lying on the floor in a pool of blood. His hands and feet were bound and he was tied to the end of his bed. It looked as if he had been beaten and then slashed with a knife. The school doctor arrived, and, after a few minutes, was able to revive Whittaker and get him up on his feet.

By this time, a few cadets and several officers had also arrived on the scene. One of them, Lieutenant Colonel Henry M. Lazelle, was the commandant in charge of cadets. General John M. Scho-

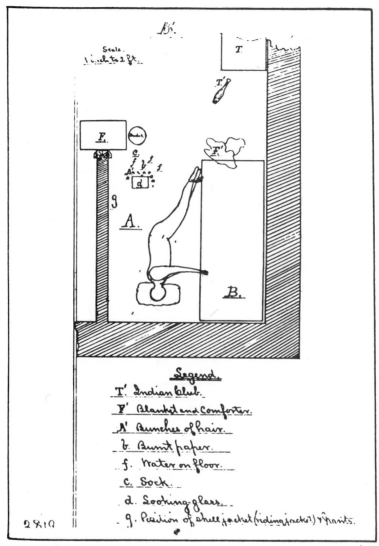

A diagram showing Whittaker's position as he was found in his room after the attack.

field, the superintendent of the academy, was on his way, because he wanted to take the situation under his personal control. In the meantime, the doctor was treating Whittaker's wounds, and both he and Colonel Lazelle were questioning the young cadet about what had happened.

Whittaker said that he had been awakened in the middle of the night to find three men, all wearing masks, standing over him. They knocked him out of bed and began beating him. Someone said, "Mark him like they do the pigs." The next thing Whittaker knew, his ears were being slashed. As he tried to protect himself, he was cut on his hand and foot. His assailants then tried to cut off his hair. Whittaker fought back, so they tied him to the foot of the bed. When the attackers had finished beating him and left, Whittaker tried to call for help, but, weak from the beating and from loss of blood, he passed out. The next thing he remembered, the doctor was reviving him.

Whittaker showed the officers a handwritten note that he said he had received on the previous day. "Mr. Whittaker," the note said, "you will be 'fixed'. Better keep awake." It was signed simply "A friend."

WEST POINT INVESTIGATES

General Schofield ordered Colonel Lazelle to conduct a full investigation of the incident, and the colonel began by questioning the doctor and many of the cadets. But no one wanted to believe that West Point cadets would inflict such a terrible beating on one of

The warning note received by Johnson Whittaker the day before the attack.

their own fellow students. Both the doctor and Colonel Lazelle believed that if the cadets would have done such a thing, it would only have been done in "the spirit of mere mischief." But all of the cadets quickly denied that they had anything to do with it. The colonel believed that his students would not be capable of committing such a dishonorable deed and then adding further dishonor by telling outright lies. Also, why would cadets harm the name of West Point by such an attack?

Therefore, when Colonel Lazelle wrote his report about the incident, he concluded that, for some unknown reason, Johnson Whittaker had written *himself* the threatening note, had beaten and slashed *himself*, and had then tied *himself* to the bed. Furthermore, because these acts were so unworthy of a West Point cadet, Colonel Lazelle recommended that Whittaker be given his choice of resigning, asking for a **court of inquiry,** or asking for a **court-martial.** When General Schofield confronted Whittaker with the results of Colonel Lazelle's investigation, the cadet insisted that the report was totally wrong, and he asked for a court of inquiry.

THE COURT OF INQUIRY

Three days after Johnson Whittaker had been found unconscious and bleeding on the floor of his room, he stood before a court inquiring into his case. A mathematics professor at West Point had been appointed to defend him.

Whittaker himself was the first witness in the case, and he was questioned in detail for a day and a half. He told his story well, reaffirmed it under **cross-examination,** and swore on the Bible that his version was true—that he had no part in the act which had been committed.

As the inquiry proceeded, the case of Johnson Whittaker attracted the attention of the nation's newspapers. Before long, it had become a controversial issue, and it eventually took on such political importance that Rutherford B. Hayes, then president of the United States, became involved in the case. President Hayes sent his own personal representative to West Point to attend the proceedings and see that the case was handled justly.

As the inquiry continued, dozens of witnesses were called, including officers, cadets, and civilians. Almost every witness disagreed with Whittaker's version of what had happened. Finally, after the inquiry had been in progress for about a month, Whittaker was called back to the witness stand. Again, he was asked detailed questions about the beating, and again he answered exactly as he had before. At the end of the cross-examination, the prosecutor stepped back, eyed Whittaker with suspicion, and asked him whether he had, in fact, written the note of warning.

"I did not," said Whittaker.

"Then why have the handwriting experts agreed that you did write the note?"

"I don't know," Whittaker answered.

The opinions of these "experts" had been submitted as **evidence,** but they had not explained how they arrived at this conclusion. After the cross-examination concerning the note, the court of inquiry came to a close.

The prosecutor summed up his case, bitterly attacking Whittaker's testimony and defending the honor of the other West Point cadets. The evidence against Whittaker was only **circumstantial;** that is, it was not direct or first-hand evidence. According to the prose-

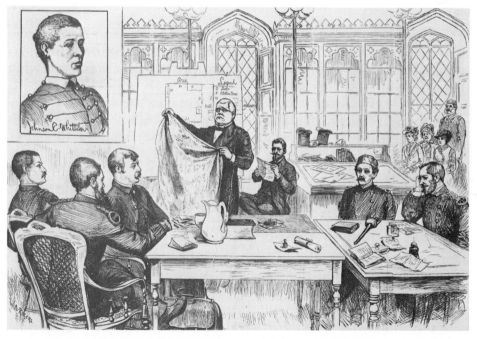

The court of inquiry that tried Johnson Whittaker.

cutor, however, it was strong enough to warrant a finding against him. "The circumstantial evidence against [Cadet Whittaker] is so strong," he concluded, "that the merits of the case stringently demand that he be tried by a General Court-Martial . . . for conduct unbecoming a Cadet and a gentleman, and for **perjury**."

The members of the court agreed, and concluded that there was enough evidence to go ahead with a court-martial. But neither West Point, the army, nor the president took any action against Johnson Whittaker. The country as a whole was not convinced of his guilt, and the issue was argued back and forth in the newspapers.

FROM THE COURT OF INQUIRY TO THE COURT-MARTIAL

In June, Whittaker took his final examination in philosophy, the course with which he had been having the most trouble. Several days later, he was informed that he had failed the exam. Months dragged by, but still nothing was done to resolve Whittaker's case. For the time being, he remained a cadet, at least officially. In the end, Johnson Whittaker was quietly given an extended leave of absence from the U.S. Military Academy at West Point. General Schofield was transferred to another post. Then, just before Christmas of 1880, President Hayes announced that a full court-martial had been scheduled, to begin after the first of the year. A full court-martial was something that not only Whittaker but also the officers and cadets of West Point had wanted. Whittaker wanted it so that he could prove his innocence and be reinstated to the military academy. The others wanted it to prove that the incident cast no blame on any person associated with West Point except Johnson Whittaker.

The court-martial began in New York City on January 20, 1881. Ten officers, most of whom had never attended West Point, were appointed to hear the case. The board was designed to be impartial, and the court-martial would be held in a courtroom away from West Point, so that no matter what the outcome, there would be no charges of prejudice. This time, Whittaker was to have professional legal assistance; Daniel H. Chamberlain, a former governor of South Carolina and a respected attorney, was appointed Whittaker's defense counsel. As the court-martial began, Johnson Whittaker appeared in court in his cadet uniform and was asked how he would plead. "Not guilty," he replied in a clear and forceful tone.

Among the first witnesses to be called to testify was General Schofield himself. The general spoke of the honor among West Point cadets, and he insisted that it was almost impossible to imagine that cadets would carry out such an act and then deny it under oath. General Schofield also admitted that he had originally believed that Whittaker had been attacked, but that he had changed his mind later. "Well," said the general, "I began to think after a while that [Whittaker] was too ready in his demand for a court of inquiry. It seemed to me . . . that he had known what was coming and that he was assured of a strong backing if he got in trouble."

But Whittaker had a good defense attorney. He thought that the general's line of reasoning was incredible, and he quickly brought that fact to the attention of the court-martial board. "Do you think that a demand for a court of inquiry was a sign of guilt?" the attorney asked, in a tone of disbelief. The general admitted that he did. Defense attorney Chamberlain then went on to accuse General Schofield of a prejudiced attitude on the subject of Whittaker's guilt or innocence. Furthermore, he pointed out that this prejudice had undoubtedly influenced the court of inquiry that had been convened under his command.

The court-martial dragged on and on. Weeks after it began, a new president, James A. Garfield, took office and was informed of the progress of the case. Many cadets were called to the witness stand to tell their stories, and all those who testified believed that Whittaker had hurt himself for his own personal reasons. Each cadet defended the "silent treatment," arguing that there was nothing wrong with it and that it had no bearing on the act that was under investigation. The West Point doctor who had originally treated Whittaker's wounds also expressed his strong belief that Whittaker was guilty. But another doctor, who had also examined Whittaker, testified that ". . . upon reflection I made up my mind that he had not done it— could not have done as brutal a thing." Handwriting experts also testified, some saying that Whittaker had written the warning note and others saying that he had not.

As the court-martial progressed, things began going a little more in Whittaker's favor than they had earlier at the court of inquiry. Several witnesses testified that Whittaker's hands had been tied very tightly, and this created some doubt as to whether he could have possibly tied himself up so effectively. On the whole, there was little evidence to show that "others" had committed the act, but there was even less evidence that Johnson Whittaker had done it himself.

JOHNSON WHITTAKER TAKES THE STAND

When it was time for the defense to present its case, Whittaker was called to the witness stand again. He repeated his version of the story and was then cross-examined by the prosecution. Whittaker stuck to his story, but now and then he did contradict himself on minor points. On the whole, however, Johnson Whittaker was a good witness in his own defense. The prosecution had made a point of stressing the honor and integrity of the West Point cadets. For his part, the defense attorney also called numerous witnesses to testify to Whittaker's good character.

For months the arguments went back and forth. The court-martial, which had begun in January, had now lasted through the first half of May. Finally, on May 17, 1881, both sides ended their cases, and the attorneys presented their closing arguments. On June 10, 1881, nearly five months from the day the court-martial had begun, the board reached its verdict. They found Johnson Whittaker guilty both of mutilating himself and of perjuring himself before the court of inquiry that had been previously conducted at West Point. The board sentenced Whittaker to a dishonorable discharge from the military academy, to a year's imprisonment, and to a fine of one dollar.

THE CASE IS REVIEWED IN WASHINGTON

Before the sentence could be carried out, however, military law required a review of Whittaker's case by the Judge Advocate General's office in Washington. In December of that year, D. G. Swain, the judge advocate general, presented the result of his review to the secretary of war. In his opinion, the verdict of the court-martial board had been totally wrong and should be reversed. Swain not only picked apart the prosecution's case, but he also argued that the court-martial itself had not been legal because President Hayes, who had ordered it, did not have the right to do so. The report of the judge advocate general passed from the secretary of war to the attorney general and finally to the president. James Garfield had been assassinated earlier that year, and the new president, Chester A. Arthur, received the report in March 1882. President Arthur overturned the conviction of Johnson Whittaker on the grounds that the court-martial itself had been illegal. He did not, however, offer an opinion as to whether Whittaker was guilty or innocent.

21

On the day that Johnson Whittaker learned that his conviction had been overturned, he also received word that he had been formally discharged from the U.S. Military Academy because of the philosophy course he had failed almost two years before. Johnson Whittaker went back to South Carolina. He finished his education there and went on to become a lawyer, a teacher, and a school administrator. He married, and the Whittakers had two sons. When the Whittaker boys were grown, they both received commissions in the U.S. Army and served as officers in World War I. Johnson Whittaker died in 1931 at the age of seventy-two, his body—and, no doubt, his heart as well—still bearing the scars he had received that night at West Point so many years ago.

Testing Your Understanding

1. Who was Johnson Whittaker? In what ways was his West Point experience different from the other cadets?

2. What explanation did Whittaker offer for the injury he suffered in April of 1880? What was Colonel Lazelle's explanation of the incident?

3. Why did West Point schedule a court of inquiry? What charges were brought and against whom?

4. What did the formal court of inquiry decide in this case? Do you think the proceeding was fair? Explain your answer.

5. More than six months after the close of the court of inquiry, a full court-martial began. Why did this happen?

6. How was the court-martial proceeding different from the court of inquiry? Was the court-martial proceeding more fair? Explain your answer.

7. Make a list of the evidence in the story that supports each side. Indicate which evidence is *direct* and which is *circumstantial*. Indicate which evidence you feel is the most believable or credible. Explain.

8. Eventually, Whittaker's conviction and punishment were overturned. How did this happen? Did Whittaker return to West Point? Why or why not?

9. Some people felt that West Point officials attempted to cover up any wrongdoing by the other cadets. Do you agree or disagree with this opinion? Why might they have engaged in a cover-up?

10. How do you think the Whittaker case reflected race relations between blacks and whites at that time?

3

John T. Scopes

BACKGROUND

The decade of the 1920s brought new ideas to traditional America. American contact with Europe following World War I increased America's awareness of global concerns. Technological innovations, such as the mass production of the inexpensive automobile, increased people's mobility. New scientific advancements, such as the development of radio and telephone, facilitated the exchange of information. Not all ideas were welcomed, however. The teachings of Karl Marx, for example, and the growth of international communism threatened American institutions.

The growth of cities and the influence of urban life also weakened traditional family patterns and changed styles of daily living. Census returns from 1920 indicated that, for the first time, fewer than half the American people lived in rural areas; most were in large towns and cities. Many Americans came to view the city as a place that nourished some questionable values. They looked with suspicion upon certain concepts and attitudes that differed from their own beliefs and traditions.

In response to the sudden changes in their ways of life, many Americans wanted to hold on to traditional values. Laws were passed in an attempt to protect these values. In 1919, the manufacture or sale of intoxicating liquor was prohibited by the Eighteenth Amendment to the U.S. Constitution. In the early '20s, several states banned the teaching of evolution. The thought of children learning the theory of evolution at the expense of a literal biblical view of human creation threatened the religious beliefs of some people. Others, however, were opposed to keeping evolution out of the schools. They saw antievolution laws as a retreat from the intellectual and political freedoms gained in the march of scientific and social progress.

THE SCOPES CASE

John T. Scopes, a high school teacher in Dayton, Tennessee, was playing tennis one spring afternoon in 1925. Midway through the game, a boy appeared to tell him he was wanted down at Robinson's Drugstore.

Dayton was a mining town of about 1,800 people in eastern Tennessee. Robinson's Drugstore was a local hangout, a place where the men of the town would meet for ice cream and soft drinks and talk about the news of the day. The men who had asked to see John Scopes were important men in Dayton, and Doc Robinson, the druggist, was chairman of the school board. So John Scopes ended his game and went off to see what they wanted.

A BIOLOGY TEACHER MAKES HISTORY

John Scopes, twenty-four years old, a slender, quiet young man with freckles, was perhaps the best-liked teacher in the school. He taught science and coached the football team. He knew the men he was going to see; he liked them and they liked him. When Scopes arrived at Doc Robinson's drugstore, his friend came right to the point. "John, we've been arguing," one of the men began, "and I said that nobody could teach biology without teaching evolution."

"That's right," Scopes said, and he took down from a shelf in the store a copy of the biology textbook used in the Dayton high school. (Doc Robinson sold textbooks as well as sodas.) He explained that this was the textbook that had been adopted by the state of Tennessee and provided to the school, and it contained a section on evolution.

"You have been teaching them this book?"

"Yes. I mean, I guess I have," Scopes answered.

"Then you have been violating the law."

THE BUTLER ACT:
PROHIBITING THE TEACHING OF EVOLUTION

The law they were talking about was called the Butler Act. John Washington Butler, a farmer and state legislator, had introduced a bill prohibiting the teaching of evolutionary theory in all public schools in Tennessee. The bill stated that "it shall be unlawful for

25

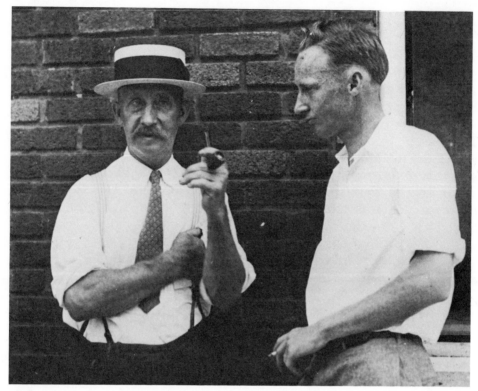

John T. Scopes, *right*, with his father.

any teacher to teach any theory that denies the story of the Divine Creation of man as taught in the Bible, and to teach instead that man has descended from a lower order of animals." The bill had passed in the state legislature and become law only a few months earlier.

Butler was a fundamentalist (a person who believes in a strictly literal interpretation of the Bible). Like all fundamentalists, he accepted the Bible as a description of historical fact, not simply as a work of religious and moral inspiration. According to the fundamentalists, the story of Adam and Eve described exactly the way human life began on earth. The evolutionary theory of Charles Darwin—that people descended from a lower order of animals (the monkeys and apes)—was certainly *not* in the Bible. Therefore, they claimed, this theory was wrong. The American Civil Liberties Union (ACLU) had heard about the Butler Act, and they were disturbed that such a law had been passed in this country. From their point of view, not allowing evolution to be taught due to objections from a particular religious group violated the U.S. Constitution. So the ACLU offered to provide lawyers and all other costs to any teacher in the state of Tennessee who would stand up and fight this "illegal" law.

TESTING THE ACT OR SAVING THE TOWN?

The men sitting around the table in Doc Robinson's drugstore that May afternoon did not completely agree or disagree with the fundamentalists. They knew that evolution was generally accepted as a valid scientific theory. On the other hand, the fundamentalists made up a large part of the population of eastern Tennessee, and they were a major political force. But it was not only the Bible or the theory of evolution that had brought these men together that afternoon. It was something much more practical: the future of their own home town. The town of Dayton was in financial trouble. The men believed that Dayton could use some publicity—and the money that a lot of publicity would bring to the town. Publicity might be just the thing to put Dayton back on the map. They turned to John Scopes and put their proposition before him. "John, would you be willing to stand for a **test case**?"

John Scopes believed in the theory of evolution and felt that the law that prohibited teaching it was wrong. On the other hand, he was not entirely sure that he wanted to be the "sacrificial lamb." But he finally agreed to take a public stand against the law. Doc Robinson went to the telephone and called the newspaper in Chattanooga. "I'm chairman of the school board here," he said. "We've just arrested a man for teaching evolution." This simple act began the chain of events that culminated in the world-famous Scopes Trial.

A NATION RESPONDS

Newspapers throughout the country picked up the story. H. L. Mencken, a famous writer in Baltimore, began to refer to the case as the *Monkey Trial* because it was concerned with the evolution of the human species from monkeys. The nickname stuck, and to this day the trial is often called the *Scopes Monkey Trial.*

A man named William Jennings Bryan also read about the upcoming trial. He wrote to state officials in Tennessee, offering his services to **prosecute** the young man who, he said, would "rob . . . children of religion and turn them out atheists." At the age of sixty-five, William Jennings Bryan was a famous orator, known throughout the world. He had served in Congress, and he had been secretary of state under President Woodrow Wilson. He had been the Democratic party's candidate for president of the United States three times, but he had lost twice to William McKinley and once to William Howard Taft. And Bryan was a confirmed fundamentalist.

Bryan's entry into the case was precisely what the men sitting in Doc Robinson's that afternoon in May had wanted. The trial in Dayton was becoming a national news event. The great and flamboyant speaker William Jennings Bryan would be coming to town on behalf of fundamentalism. He would undoubtedly put on quite a show. His fame overshadowed the fact that he had not tried a case in court for almost forty years.

Another famous American also heard about the trial, and he was as opposed to fundamentalism as Bryan was in favor of it. His name was Clarence Darrow, and he offered to defend John Scopes. In 1925, the sixty-eight-year-old Darrow was the most famous criminal lawyer of his time. Only a year earlier, he had defended Nathan Leopold and Richard Loeb in their sensational trial for the murder of young Bobby Franks, and he had succeeded in saving them from the death sentence. Scopes knew that with a world-famous figure like Bryan prosecuting him, he would need a top lawyer to take charge of his defense. He gladly accepted Darrow's offer.

William Jennings Bryan

PREPARING FOR THE TRIAL

The trial was set for July 10, 1925, and it was discussed not only in the United States but in Europe as well. It was truly the news of the day. After the Fourth of July holiday, thousands of people began to pour into Dayton, a little town with a normal population of only 1,800. More than 100 newspaper reporters arrived to cover the trial, and Western Union sent 22 telegraph operators just to relay the reporters' stories to their home offices around the country.

The town of Dayton had gotten just what it wanted. And the town was prepared for its sudden fame. The "monkey trial" nickname had caught on, and the stores were selling stuffed monkeys as souvenirs. Trained chimpanzees were even brought into town to perform. The word *monkey* was attached to almost anything that could be sold. There were bands, sideshows, refreshment stands, parades, street-corner preachers, and revival meetings. One store owner was lucky enough to profit by his name. He hung this sign in his window:

DARWIN IS RIGHT—INSIDE

H. L. Mencken called the town a "universal joke."

In the days just before the trial, John Scopes went back to his home in Paducah, Kentucky, hoping to relax there before the ordeal that faced him. One day, however, Doc Robinson called him and said he had better get back to Dayton. There had been a shooting in town and the reason for it was an argument about evolution. If Scopes was back in town, they could perhaps keep things calm, Doc Robinson said. So Scopes returned. Once back, however, he discovered that the shooting had been a fake. The participants had fired at each other all right—with blanks. It had just been another publicity stunt to help get Dayton "back on the map." John Scopes was furious.

BRYAN VS. DARROW: THE TRIAL HEATS UP

The morning of July 10 was brutally hot and humid—a typical summer day in eastern Tennessee. The courtroom (which had been rebuilt to seat more than 600 people) filled quickly. Almost everyone was in shirtsleeves and most were already fanning themselves. Presiding over the trial was Judge John Tate Raulston from the town of Gizzards Cove, Tennessee. The most conspicuous figure at the

Clarence Darrow

defense table was Clarence Darrow. Everything about him was baggy and rumpled: his pants, his shirt, and even his jowls. He wore bright purple suspenders (his trademark) and wire-rimmed glasses that kept sliding down his nose. His movements were slow and deliberate, even as he sat there fanning himself in the stifling heat. With Darrow were the other members of the **defense** team: Dudley Field Malone and Arthur Garfield Hays (two of the nation's top lawyers), who had arrived with Darrow, and John Randolph Neal (dean of a Tennessee law school), a friend of Scopes.

Bryan sat at the prosecution table, fanning himself, too. He was overweight and looked tired. He no longer resembled the tremendously energetic and fiery speaker he had been in younger days, when he had campaigned all over the country for the presidency. But he said he was ready and that he planned to deliver what would be perhaps the best speech of his life. Bryan had insisted that the *Scopes* case concerned "the right of the people, speaking through the legislature, to control the schools which they create and support."

30

THE EVIDENCE

As the trial began, the defense tried to answer this argument. They said that the case was about "freedom of teaching" and "freedom of learning." "If today you can take a thing like evolution and make it a crime to teach it in the public schools," said Darrow, "tomorrow you can make it a crime to teach it in the private schools. . . . At the next session, you may ban it in books and newspapers. . . . After a while, your Honor, it is the setting of man against man and creed against creed until with flying banners and beating drums we are marching backward to the glorious ages of the sixteenth century. . . ."

After the **opening arguments** of both sides, the prosecution heard **testimony** from several of Scopes's students. The boys admitted that Scopes had taught the theory of evolution. Suddenly, the prosecution rested its case. Apparently, Bryan was planning to save until later the speech that he said would be the best of his career.

Darrow began his case by announcing that he would like to bring certain scientists and other scholars before the court to explain the theory of evolution. He wanted to show that the theory of evolution did not "deny the story of divine creation as taught in the Bible." If there was no contradiction between evolution and creation, then Scopes had not violated the law.

William Jennings Bryan argued against allowing expert witnesses to testify about religion and evolution. But it was soon clear that his argument was not completely a legal argument. Instead it was a fundamentalist sermon that really belonged in a church, not a courtroom. The audience responded to Bryan's speech as if they too were in church. At the proper times, they would say "Amen" or "Praise be to the Lord!" When Bryan finished, he slumped back in his chair, deeply satisfied. The audience in the courtroom applauded.

Dudley Field Malone, one of the defense lawyers (who had once worked for Bryan), rose to answer the prosecutor. His speech was masterful, and the large audience sat in silent attention, listening to every word. As he came to a close, Malone said: "The least that this generation can do . . . is to give the next generation all the facts, all the available data, all the theories, all the information that learning, that study, that observation has produced; give it to the children in the hope to heaven that they will make a better world of this than we have been able to make of it. . . . We do not fear all the truth. . . . We feel we stand with progress . . . with science . . . with intelligence. We feel we stand with fundamental freedom in America. We are not afraid. Where is the fear? We meet it! Where is the fear? We defy it!"

When Malone finished his speech, hundreds of people in the courtroom stood and cheered. Chaos broke out, and Judge Raulston cleared the court. Soon, the only people left in the courtroom were the judge, the lawyers, and John Scopes. William Jennings Bryan sat there as if he had been hit across the chest with a board. He turned to his former employee and said in a soft voice, "Dudley, that was the greatest speech I have ever heard."

The court then made its decision on expert witnesses. It refused to grant Darrow's request. Judge Raulston said that the trial was only concerned with whether or not John Scopes had taught that man was descended from lower forms of animals. That, he felt, was what the statute prohibited. Technically, the small-town judge was correct.

WILLIAM JENNINGS BRYAN TAKES THE STAND

On the seventh day, Judge Raulston moved the entire trial outside onto the courthouse lawn because of the intense heat. Clarence Darrow seemed to be in a difficult position. His entire strategy— that of bringing scientists and scholars to the witness stand—had been denied. Some said that Darrow no longer had a case. But they underestimated the brilliant trial lawyer. When the trial proceeded, Darrow approached the judge and said: "The defense desires to call Mr. William Jennings Bryan as a witness."

Bryan was taken by surprise, but he did not object. He took the witness stand. "Do you claim that everything in the Bible should be literally interpreted?" Darrow asked.

"I believe everything in the Bible should be accepted as it is given there. Some of the Bible is given illustratively, for instance: 'Ye are the salt of the earth.' I would not insist that man was actually salt. . ."

"But when you read that Jonah swallowed the whale—or that the whale swallowed Jonah—excuse me, please; how do you interpret that?"

"I read that a big fish swallowed Jonah. It does not say 'whale.' "

Darrow saw that Bryan was trying to avoid conflicts between the language of the Bible and scientific knowledge that would suggest that words in the Bible could also have symbolic meaning. It was just what he had wanted. "Now, you say that the big fish swallowed Jonah and he remained there—how long?—three days, and then it spewed him up on the land? You believe that the big fish was made to swallow Jonah?"

"I am not prepared to say that; the Bible merely says it was done."

Darrow moved on to other things. Had Joshua really made the sun stand still? What would happen if the earth *did* stand still? Was the date of creation really 4004 B.C., as one version of the Bible claimed? In response to that question, Bryan answered that he believed it but had never really thought about it.

"What *do* you think?" Darrow asked sarcastically.

"I do not think about things that I don't think about," Bryan replied.

"Well, do you think about things that you *do* think about?"

"Well, sometimes," Bryan answered.

The audience burst into laughter. The great William Jennings Bryan was making a fool of himself. The questioning continued.

The jury listens to the arguments during the Scopes trial.

Darrow asked the questions, and Bryan himself became embarrassed with his answers.

"Do you think the earth was made in six days?" Darrow asked.

"Not six days of twenty-four hours."

"Doesn't the Bible say so?"

By this time, Bryan was becoming confused. "No, sir," he answered. The fundamentalists were shocked at his answer. They believed that it *was* six days of twenty-four hours each. In discussing the story of creation, Darrow mentioned that the serpent was punished by God for its part in the temptation of Adam. "Do you think that is why the serpent is compelled to crawl upon its belly?" asked Darrow.

"I believe that," Bryan replied.

"Have you any idea how the snake moved about before that time?" Darrow continued.

"No, sir."

"Do you know whether he walked on his tail or not?" Again there was laughter. The people were now laughing *at* William Jennings Bryan, not at Darrow's questions. Finally, in desperation, Bryan shouted in anger: "The only purpose Mr. Darrow has is to slur at the Bible. . . . I want the world to know that this man, who does not believe in a God, is trying to use a court in Tennessee . . ."

"I object to that," Darrow yelled back. "I am examining you on your fool ideas that no intelligent Christian on earth believes."

Judge Raulston cooled their tempers by announcing that court was adjourned for the day. Bryan's agonizing and embarrassing hours were over. Bryan had not persuaded the world to accept his beliefs. Instead, he had ended up having made a fool of himself. Bryan was a tired and defeated man as he went back to the hotel that evening. Almost everyone in the United States would know it, too, when they read the newspaper accounts of his testimony.

THE VERDICT

The next day, the trial came to an end. Darrow, to prevent giving Bryan the chance to make his "great speech," asked the judge to skip the **closing arguments.** All that there was to say had already been said. The judge agreed and turned the case directly over to the jury. Scopes was quickly found guilty, and the judge fined him $100. Of course, the jury was right: Scopes was technically guilty of violating Tennessee law. But the reasonableness of that law was drawn into question.

Five days after the trial, while still in Dayton, William Jennings Bryan died as he was writing down the great speech he had never made. Clarence Darrow went on to try other cases. John Scopes continued his education and later became a geologist. The souvenirs and trained chimpanzees disappeared.

The town of Dayton once again became a quiet little southern community, where hardly anything exciting ever happened. Once again, the high points of the day were those friendly little meetings in Doc Robinson's drugstore.

Testing Your Understanding

1. How did the Butler Act restrict the teaching of biology in Tennessee high schools?

2. What is the difference between evolution and divine creation?

3. What is meant by a *test case?* Why does the Scopes trial qualify as one?

4. What interest did William Jennings Bryan have in coming to eastern Tennessee? What interest did Clarence Darrow have? How did each go about his task, and with what success?

5. Some commentators have noted that although Scopes lost the decision, his belief in the right to teach evolution was upheld. Do you agree or disagree? Why?

6. Many people have an interest in public education. These people include students, parents, teachers, administrators, school board members, state education authorities, and other members of the community. Who decided what was taught in the Dayton, Tennessee, school? Who should decide what is taught in the schools? What process should be used?

7. In the 1980s, people are still concerned about whether schools should teach evolution, the biblical story of creation, or both. How would you resolve this dilemma? Give reasons for your answer.

4
General
Billy Mitchell

BACKGROUND

In an era when nations of the world are talking about the use of weapons in space, it is interesting to remember that no more than seventy years ago war was limited to land and sea battles. At the start of World War I, for instance, airplanes were a recent invention and were used mostly to observe enemy troop movements on the ground. As the war continued, airplanes became more directly involved in combat. They were armed with machine guns and bombs and were used against other airpianes as well as against ground troops and supply centers.

Billy Mitchell, a young army major, came to France in 1917 with the American forces to join the fight against Germany. The son of a U.S. senator and a daring man of action, Mitchell believed in the importance of the airplane in modern warfare. On the front lines, he commanded the first squadrons of American airmen in combat. Mitchell became a hero by flying alone behind enemy lines to discover the direction of a major German attack. His information helped the Allies stop the German advance and turn the tide of the war. Behind the scenes, Mitchell wrote letters to friends in Washington, D.C., to gain support for the air corps. In less than two years, Mitchell was made brigadier general.

Mitchell and his airmen were heroes when they returned victoriously from the European war. The mood of the nation, though, soon changed from war to peace. The highest-ranking military officers lost interest in the airplane as a weapon. Mitchell, however, had other ideas. He believed that our surrounding oceans would no longer isolate America from foreign enemies because of possible enemy attack by air. Mitchell proposed a system of national defense based on airplanes instead of more costly and less mobile ships and forts.

Mitchell also believed that modern warfare required a central government agency for all our armed forces. Until then, there had been a Department of War for the army and a Department of Navy. Mitchell proposed to join these two departments and add an air force as a third branch under a Department of National Defense. When his superiors did not approve these ideas, Mitchell took his case to Congress and to the public. He testified in hearings on Capitol Hill and wrote articles in popular magazines.

Mitchell's superiors were angry that he attempted to go around their authority. They were upset when he told the press that neglect by top military leaders had caused a series of fatal crashes of military aircraft. His superiors believed that it was a violation of military discipline for Mitchell to criticize them in public.

The First Amendment to the U.S. Constitution protects everyone's freedom of speech. In the military, however, freedom of speech may come into conflict with military needs and the duty to obey orders. Mitchell had always taken great personal risks in the line of duty and was ready to take another. He believed that public debate on the issue of the future of air power was in the best interest of the country.

THE MITCHELL CASE

A small fleet of heavily armored German warships rolled with the sea in the waters of the Atlantic Ocean, just off the coast of Norfolk, Virginia. There was a U-boat (one of the devastating German submarines), a destroyer, a cruiser, and the *Ostfriesland*, one of Germany's most powerful battleships, a vessel so strongly built that many said it was absolutely unsinkable. Suddenly, a force of small biplanes appeared in the skies, struggling and weaving under heavy loads of bombs. One by one, the planes headed for the German warships.

The attack of the small planes was not an act of war. The time was June 1921, and World War I had been over for three years. Germany no longer even *had* a military force. The bomb-laden airplanes were being used in a kind of experiment. The ships, which

The German battleship *Ostfriesland* slowly sinks after being bombed by Mitchell's planes.

had been captured from the German navy, were actually a "ghost fleet": their engines were shut down and there was not a man aboard any of them.

The demonstration was being staged by Brigadier General Billy Mitchell, the most successful American air commander of World War I. General Mitchell had been the first officer to command planes that actually took part in combat. Until then, air power had only been used for scouting, spying, and other noncombat missions. General Mitchell's planes had been quite successful in the war effort, yet after the war was over, the air corps was still only a minor subdivision of the army. Its planes were thin-skinned, wobbly, and small. The air corps was simply not considered very important by either the army or the navy. General Billy Mitchell, who was much more of an "airman" than an "army man," did not share this opinion at all. He believed that the air corps was not simply an important fighting unit but that, in the future, it was going to be the *most* important military force.

BILLY MITCHELL TAKES HIS CASE TO CONGRESS

After the war, Mitchell went before Congress and explained that air power was even greater than sea power, because airplanes could sink any naval ship by bombing it. High-ranking officers of the navy ridiculed him for this statement. Josephus Daniels, secretary of the navy, boasted that he would not be afraid to "stand bareheaded on the deck of a battleship and let Brigadier General Mitchell take a crack at me with a bombing airplane." Mitchell replied that he could prove his statement if he had some ships to bomb. So the captured German ships were provided as targets, and the test was arranged.

General Mitchell himself directed the attack on the German warships from his own plane, while other military leaders, government officials, and various congressmen watched from the shore. Millions of other people throughout the United States were also awaiting the outcome of the test. General Billy Mitchell's operation had by now become a topic of great national interest. After Mitchell's planes arrived at the target area, they dove to the attack. One after the other, the small biplanes unleashed their bombs at the ships. First, the submarine went under, then the destroyer and the cruiser keeled over and sank. Finally, the mighty German battleship *Ostfriesland,* brutally damaged, raised its bow to the sky and, like a great broad-blade sword, slid into the sea.

THE NAVY'S REACTION

The navy officers and officials were stunned. General Mitchell had proven the might of air power beyond their expectations. But still they refused to give in. While they had to admit that airplanes could sink unarmed, unmanned ships anchored at sea, they believed that fully armed ships under the command of naval officers and experienced sailors would produce a completely different outcome. In a fair fight, they insisted, Billy Mitchell's air power would be soundly defeated.

Mitchell believed that unarmed ships were actually harder to sink. He said that ships were most often sunk when a bomb or shell struck the ship's own ammunition supply, causing a much bigger explosion. The ships sunk by his planes were destroyed by bombs alone.

The congressmen and government officials in Washington seemed to think that the navy's argument had been correct. It appeared that Mitchell had not won the dispute, in spite of the success of his experiment. As time went on, nothing was done to enlarge or modernize the air corps, but General Mitchell refused to give up. He continued to take his case for a strong and separate air force to both the government and the people of the United States. But the officials of the Department of War grew tired of Mitchell's campaign, and they transferred him to San Antonio, Texas.

THE CRASH OF THE *SHENANDOAH*

Four years passed. Then several air tragedies occurred that shocked the nation. The worst of these tragedies involved a navy dirigible named the *Shenandoah,* which had been caught in a severe storm. The ship was torn in half, and many members of its crew fell thousands of feet to their deaths; fourteen men died in the accident. Word leaked out that the airship might not have been in a safe flying condition but that the navy had ordered it to be flown anyway. The navy ignored this rumor and announced instead that the bright side of the accident was that it showed clearly that we had little to fear from an "airborne enemy." Flying craft could not even weather a storm, said the navy. How could it survive an attack by the antiaircraft guns of a navy ship?

This was too much for General Billy Mitchell. He conducted his own investigation of the accident itself and then held a press con-

A crowd gathers around the wreckage of the *Shenandoah* after its crash.

ference in San Antonio where he announced that the accidents were a "direct result of incompetency, **criminal negligence,** and almost **treasonable** administration by the War and Navy Departments." General Mitchell was back on the front pages of almost every major newspaper in the United States. His statement was powerful and shocking, one that the average military officer would not dare to make in public about his superiors. Military officials were horrified, but at the same time, they were pleased. Now they had a *real* offense with which to get back at their long-time critic.

THE COURT-MARTIAL OF BILLY MITCHELL

Billy Mitchell had expected his superiors to react as they did, and he was prepared for trouble. As he had anticipated, he was soon ordered to stand trial before a general **court-martial.** His first act was to engage Frank R. Reid, a civilian attorney, to represent him as defense counsel. No less than eight charges were placed against

Mitchell, all expressing the ideas that his statement had been damaging to good order (and to proper military discipline) and that his conduct was "of a nature to bring discredit upon military service. . . ." The court-martial consisted of four other major generals and six brigadier generals. One member of the board was forty-five-year-old Major General Douglas MacArthur, a personal friend of Mitchell's.

The court-martial began on October 28, 1925, in Washington, D.C., with Major General Charles P. Summerall presiding. As one of his first acts, Mitchell's lawyer challenged not only two members of the board but also the presiding officer, General Summerall himself. He charged that these officers were prejudiced against Mitchell, and he was successful in having all three of them removed from the court-martial board.

The court-martial of Billy Mitchell had attracted the attention of the entire country, and several prominent persons from many walks of life were scheduled to take part. The **prosecution** would put the famous explorer Admiral Richard Byrd on the stand, while the defense planned to call Eddie Rickenbacker, World War I's greatest American pilot; the fiery congressman Fiorello La Guardia (later to become one of New York City's most famous mayors); and Will

Billy Mitchell in a Thomas More pursuit plane.

Rogers, the nation's most popular comedian, to testify on Billy Mitchell's behalf.

The prosecution's task was simple. No one denied that General Mitchell had made the shocking and critical statements attributed to him. In fact, Mitchell himself readily admitted it. Since all the charges against him stemmed from those statements, the main thrust of the trial would be the defense's efforts to show that Mitchell had been correct and that his criticism of the War Department officials had been fair and just.

Defense attorney Reid stated at the very beginning that he intended to show that Mitchell's statements were true, and that they could not be considered **libelous** on two other grounds. First, the statements were directed at the War Department, not at an individual, and libel cannot be committed against a non-living thing. And second, officers have the right to enjoy the **freedom of speech** guaranteed under the First Amendment to the U.S. Constitution, so long as they do not use this freedom to violate national security. Then, Reid announced that he intended to call more than seventy witnesses to the stand in order to prove that General Billy Mitchell was innocent. Everyone prepared for a very long trial.

One of the first witnesses called by the defense was the wife of the captain of the *Shenandoah,* the navy dirigible that had been destroyed in a storm. She testified that her husband had been unwilling to fly the dirigible because he believed it was not in safe condition. He had expressed his fears and objections to his superiors, but they ordered him to fly the mission anyway. Being a good officer, the captain had obeyed his orders. This was startling testimony, because the secretary of the navy had previously told reporters that the captain had made *no* protest at all. The captain's wife added that a navy representative had been to see her only a short while earlier and had presented her with a written statement that they wanted her to make, a statement that upheld the navy's side of the story. By revealing the navy's effort to control her testimony, she made her appearance in court even more damaging to the navy.

Next to testify was a long series of air corps officers. They expressed their belief in the importance of air power for the future security of the United States, the army's overwhelming lack of interest in this power, and the terribly poor situation into which the air corps had been allowed to degenerate. Now, what seemed to be on trial was the government's entire policy of national defense, and the individual named Billy Mitchell seemed almost forgotten. The questions came and went. Which was more valuable in defense, a navy or an air force? Which could harm an enemy more: being bombed by airplanes or being shot at by the artillery and the infantry? Was it really true that the airplane was "shrinking" the world, and that other forms of transportation, like the ship, would take a back seat because of this? In 1925, this last question was difficult to answer. Charles Lindbergh's historic nonstop flight across the Atlantic was still another year and a half in the future.

GENERAL MITCHELL IN HIS OWN DEFENSE

Finally, General Billy Mitchell took the stand. He described the great potential that he envisioned for an air force in the nation's defense. He told of the endless difficulties he had experienced in attempting to further the cause of a U.S. air force. He described how the air corps of the day was not simply at a standstill but was actually deteriorating. And he explained why he believed that the United States could be properly defended only if it had an air force provided with the proper equipment and manpower.

Then Mitchell was **cross-examined** by the prosecuting attorney. The prosecution wanted to show that Mitchell was describing not facts but merely opinions and that his statements were only prophecies that might—or might not—come true. The prosecutor tried

Billy Mitchell stands during the court-martial in 1925.

desperately to make General Mitchell appear eccentric, an oddball like those people who wander the streets preaching that the world will end tomorrow. This was not the kind of man the military needed for the task of defending the nation, said the prosecution. Dreamers, screwballs, and fanatics were not the type of people who should determine the defense policy of the United States. This was not, of course, the issue that was supposed to be decided at the trial. But then, neither was the matter of American defense policy, which Mitchell and his lawyer had introduced. According to the law, the central issue of the trial should have been simply whether Billy Mitchell was guilty or innocent of the charges against him.

THE VERDICT

From the outset of the trial, the defense had had serious problems. The generals sitting in judgment at the court-martial believed that, under the existing policies of the armed forces, Mitchell should not have made those statements, and under no circumstances should he have criticized his superiors in public. Such behavior was considered dishonorable and disgraceful in military life. Whether his motivation was right or not or whether his remarks were correct or incorrect was, in their view, beside the point. After all their many years of training and military discipline, the officers believed that Billy Mitchell simply should not have said what he did.

When the court-martial came to a close, the generals met in private to decide the question of Billy Mitchell's guilt or innocence. Not surprisingly, they found him guilty as charged. General Billy Mitchell was suspended from the army for five years.

BILLY MITCHELL'S CAMPAIGN CONTINUES

As a civilian, Billy Mitchell continued to campaign vigorously for an effective air force. Although he was never allowed to reenter the army, he saw the U.S. Air Force grow, although quite slowly, during the early 1930s. In February 1936, ten years after he had left the army, Billy Mitchell died. He had recognized the importance of air power in modern warfare and had correctly predicted that it would become the most powerful weapon yet devised. And he even predicted that the U.S. Navy would one day be in serious danger of air attack. Less than six years after Billy Mitchell died, the Japanese successfully bombed the navy ships at Pearl Harbor, an act that crippled the nation's Pacific fleet and led to America's entry into World War II.

Billy Mitchell did not live to see many of his predictions come true, but no one today questions the importance of air power. Pearl Harbor, the German *Blitzkrieg*, the allied bombings of Europe, the atomic bombs dropped on Hiroshima and Nagasaki, and the immense use of air power in Korea and Vietnam all testify to the significance of air power in modern warfare. Although Billy Mitchell was found guilty, we know today that what he said was correct and that those who brought him to trial, and those who testified against him, were proved wrong by the events of history.

Testing Your Understanding

1. Who was Billy Mitchell? Why did he bomb the ships that had been captured from the German navy?

2. What was the government's reaction to his sinking of the ships? Did the government change its policy about military air power?

3. Why did Mitchell conduct his own investigation of the crash of the *Shenandoah*?

4. Why was he court-martialed? What charges were brought against him?

5. How did he defend against the charges? Why did he defend himself as he did?

6. What was the outcome of the court-martial? Do you agree or disagree with the decision?

7. Should a military officer have the same First Amendment rights to criticize the government as citizens who are not in the military? Give reasons for your answer.

8. To what extent did Mitchell succeed in convincing the government of the importance of air power? Are there other methods he could have used to influence the government?

5

Scottsboro Nine

BACKGROUND

The roots of the Scottsboro case go deep into American history. The federal government ended Reconstruction in the South in 1877 when it returned control of state and local governments to the former Confederate states. This meant that the people of those southern states were again free to elect their own officials and govern themselves. It also meant that the enforcement of federally granted civil and voting rights for the newly freed slaves was left to the states.

These new state governments rapidly came to be dominated by the white majority. Participation of blacks in southern state and local governments declined. Although the Fifteenth Amendment guaranteed former slaves the right to vote, literacy tests and poll taxes sharply reduced the number of blacks who were eligible to vote. Disadvantaged educationally and economically because of slavery, blacks were affected more severely than whites by these measures. By the turn of the twentieth century, only a handful of black officeholders and a few voters remained.

Participation of blacks in the systems of law enforcement in the southern states also decreased after Reconstruction. Since there were few eligible black voters, blacks were rarely elected as judges, sheriffs, or district attorneys. White officials seldom appointed blacks to these positions. Methods of jury selection were controlled by white officials, who almost always kept blacks from serving on juries.

Blacks were generally at the mercy of the white-controlled governments and law enforcement systems. Because of their poverty, most blacks could not afford lawyers for their defense when they were accused of crimes. Although the Sixth Amendment to the U.S. Constitution guaranteed persons accused of a federal crime "the assistance of counsel for their defense," this did not help many people. The Supreme Court said that this amendment meant only that a person had a right to hire a lawyer, not that the trial judge had to provide one free of charge. In addition, this amendment did not apply to state courts, where most criminal trials took place. In fact, the Supreme Court rarely interfered with any decision made by state courts in a criminal case.

But if blacks did not have access to perfect justice in the courts, there was one practice that was worse. "Lynch law," where a mob of people punished a person suspected of a crime without resorting to the courts, was most frequently afflicted upon blacks. Of the twenty-one persons who died by lynching in 1930, for example, twenty were black. Lynching not only denied blacks the protection of the law, but also created an atmosphere of violence in which blacks were often deterred from asserting their rights.

When nine young black men were arrested and charged with raping two white women in 1931, an explosive situation developed in the town of Scottsboro, Alabama. A mob of angry citizens waited outside the jail and courthouse day and night while the nine were brought swiftly to trial. Later, people throughout the country would ask if justice could be done in a racially divided land.

THE SCOTTSBORO CASE

Trials were going on in the small town of Scottsboro, Alabama, in April 1931, and there was not an empty seat in the courtroom.

Outside, National Guard troops were on duty around the courthouse doors and at other key places. The guardsmen looked out at a crowd of thousands of men, women, and children. Some of those people had traveled as far as 100 miles to be a part of the noisy crowd. Music and announcements blared out from loudspeakers, and the whole atmosphere seemed more like that of a state fair than that of a legal proceeding.

ON TRIAL FOR THEIR LIVES

Inside the courtroom, however, everyone was deadly serious. Nine youths, all black and ranging in age from twelve to nineteen, were on trial for their lives. Witnesses for both the prosecution and for the defense had testified, and the trials were winding down to their close.

A lawyer summing up one case for the prosecution looked directly at the jury and said bitterly, "Guilty or not guilty, let's get rid of these niggers."

In some ways the nine accused youths could probably consider themselves lucky just to be in that courtroom and on trial. The year was 1931, in the middle of a great depression. The place was in the poverty-stricken rural South where blacks were generally treated as inferior to whites. The nine youths were accused of raping two white women, perhaps the most horrid of crimes in the mind of the average white southerner at that time. All those things combined to create the setting for a very dangerous situation. **Lynching** as an unofficial "punishment" of blacks accused of crimes against white people and their property was not uncommon in the South during those days. The armed national guardsmen surrounding the courthouse were grim reminders of the possibility of violent mob action.

The Scottsboro nine under guard in Scottsboro. They are, *from left to right*, Clarence Norris, Olen Montgomery, Andrew Wright, Willie Roberson, Ozie Powell, Eugene Williams, Charley Weems, Roy Wright, and Haywood Patterson.

49

Although the guardsmen were there to protect the nine black youths from a lynch mob during the trial, the *kind* of trial that they would get could not be guaranteed by military force. The right to a fair trial is guaranteed by the U.S. Constitution, but minority groups and the poor have sometimes been deprived of that right in one way or another. The Scottsboro nine fell into that unfortunate category. Their case was to become one of the truly disgraceful examples of an unfair trial in American history.

RIDING THE RAILS

The story of the Scottsboro nine began in March 1931. At that time, hoboes and other unemployed wanderers were a common sight all over the country. There were so many that the railroads all but gave up trying to keep them from hitching rides on freight trains. A freight train traveling through northern Alabama had its share of these nonpaying passengers, and at one point a fight broke out in a boxcar between some white youths and a group of young blacks. The blacks won the fight and forced the white youths off the moving train. But the whites complained to a local stationmaster and said they wanted to file legal charges for **assault.** The stationmaster wired ahead to a local sheriff with information about the complaint.

When the train pulled into the small town of Paint Rock, Alabama, it was met by a large group of armed men. Most had been hurriedly **deputized**—designated as sheriff's officers—while they were waiting for the train. They swarmed onto the freight train and began going through it, boxcar by boxcar. When they finished, nine black males, a white male, and two white females, all dressed in dingy coveralls and work clothes, had been taken off.

A RAPE IS REPORTED

The three white youths were left to themselves. But a deputy sheriff saw to it that the nine blacks were roped together and loaded on a truck to be taken into Scottsboro. As the truck was about to leave, one of the white females approached a deputy sheriff and calmly told him that she and her friend had been **raped** by the black youths. All the deputies standing near the truck were first stunned, and then enraged. Fortunately, some common sense prevailed, and the truck started off to Scottsboro with its nine prisoners. The dep-

A crowd gathers outside the courthouse during the trial of the Scottsboro nine.

uty sheriff in charge realized that he had a very explosive case to handle. He put the two females in a car, and they also headed into Scottsboro.

Once there, the females were sent to a doctor to be examined, and word spread through the town about the alleged rape. The Scottsboro nine were locked up in the jail, and the sheriff and his deputies settled down to see how the people would react. By nightfall, several hundred people had gathered in front of the jail, and their mood was far from calm. The situation soon became difficult to control—lynching was a real possibility. From behind the barricaded doors, the sheriff called the governor of Alabama and asked for National Guard troops to protect the nine prisoners and help keep order.

ON TRIAL IN SCOTTSBORO

While under the protection of the National Guard, the nine black youths—Haywood Patterson, Olen Montgomery, Charley Weems, Clarence Norris, Willie Roberson, Ozie Powell, Eugene Williams, and Roy and Andrew Wright—eventually went on trial. The judge in charge of the case gave the defendants little chance to contact their families or friends or to hire their own lawyers. Since they could not afford a lawyer, the nine were to be represented by a lawyer from

Chattanooga, Tennessee, sent by concerned black ministers from that city who had heard about the case, and a volunteer attorney from Scottsboro. The judge assigned these lawyers on the very morning of the trial.

When the cases were brought to trial, the two females who had been on the train, Victoria Price and Ruby Bates, went to the witness stand and described in detail how they had been raped. There were, however, many contradictions in what they said. Moreover, statements by the two doctors who had examined them did not back up their claim that each had been raped six times. Another fact brought out in court was that one of the accused males was so disabled by venereal disease that it would have been almost impossible for him to have committed the act.

A SENTENCE OF DEATH

In such trials in the South at that time, however, a verdict of "guilty" was surely predictable and not long in coming. Eight of the nine were found guilty and sentenced to death. One, Roy Wright, also was found guilty, but because he was just twelve years old, the prosecution asked that he only be given a life sentence. Still, seven members of the jury refused to accept any sentence less than death so a **mistrial** was called in the case of the twelve-year-old.

The white citizens of Scottsboro and the surrounding countryside were satisfied; they had "gotten those niggers," guilty or not guilty. Soon, however, protests began coming into Alabama from people not only in all parts of the United States but also in foreign countries. Individuals, organizations, and institutions claimed that justice had not been done. They demanded new trials and, this time, they insisted, *fair* trials. In Alabama, the reaction to these protests could only be described as puzzlement. "What's all the fuss about?" was the question some Alabamans were asking.

THE APPEALS BEGIN

When the time came for an **appeal** of the case, the International Labor Defense (ILD), which was a branch of the Communist party in the United States, and the National Association for the Advancement of Colored People (NAACP) fought over which organization would represent the Scottsboro nine. The ILD won out and appealed to the Alabama Supreme Court in early 1932. But the appeal was rejected.

The ILD then took the case of the Scottsboro nine to the U.S. Supreme Court, saying that the state of Alabama had violated the U.S. Constitution in several ways. First, the organization's lawyers claimed that the nine youths on trial in a **capital punishment** case had not been granted fair and impartial trials. Secondly, they claimed that the volunteer lawyers at the trial did not have enough time to prepare a proper defense. In other words, the Scottsboro nine did not have "effective assistance of counsel." In addition, they argued that the trials should be considered unconstitutional because blacks were automatically excluded from the **juries** that convicted the Scottsboro nine, as well as from all Alabama juries.

The Court agreed to review the case, but only on the subject of the defendants' **right to counsel.** Lawyers for Alabama argued that, under the U.S. Constitution and prior Supreme Court decisions, states should not be restricted in the way they conduct trials so long as they do not discriminate or act in an arbitrary manner. Alabama, they said, gave the defendants a trial and also gave them attorneys who did the best they could.

Haywood Patterson, *center*, sitting with his attorney, Samuel Leibowitz, *left*, holds a horseshoe and rabbit's foot for luck.

THE SUPREME COURT'S FIRST DECISION

In its majority opinion, the Supreme Court held that the U.S. Constitution did guarantee the right to counsel in state proceedings where capital punishment could be the sentence. The Fourteenth Amendment, the Court noted, provided that a state "shall not deprive any person of life, liberty, or property without **due process of law**. . . ." The Court ruled that the trial judge did not give the defendants a reasonable time to hire lawyers and that, when the judge finally asked lawyers to volunteer, there was not enough time to prepare a defense. As a result, the defendants had in effect been deprived of their right to "due process of law." The Court then ordered new trials.

The ILD obtained Samuel Leibowitz, probably the finest criminal lawyer in New York at that time, to defend the nine young men. Leibowitz agreed to take their case free of charge, but demanded it be known that his taking the case in no way meant that he subscribed to the social or political views of the ILD. He said that the case was basically one of human rights, and that he was undertaking the defense only because of his commitment to these rights.

RETRIALS WITH EFFECTIVE COUNSEL

The new trials were scheduled to take place at Decatur, Alabama, under a new judge, James E. Horton. The time was set for March 1933, two years after the alleged rape incident. Samuel Leibowitz, the defense lawyer, was clever and intelligent, well known for his dramatic courtroom performances and for the power of his relentless **cross-examination** of witnesses. From the beginning, he felt that there was one major issue in the Scottsboro case that would eventually have to be settled. Because black people were kept off **jury lists** in Alabama, they therefore would never be called to sit on a jury. Leibowitz believed this was unconstitutional and, more appropriate to his present task, grounds for appeal if he lost the Scottsboro case in Alabama. He emphasized this point in the selection of a jury, even though he knew no blacks would be allowed on the jury.

The main witness of the prosecution was once again Victoria Price, the young woman who, at the first trial, had been presented not only as an innocent victim of a horrible crime but also as a

Victoria Price   Ruby Bates

proud example of white southern womanhood. Again, she told the story of how she and Ruby Bates had been assaulted on that fateful day some two years earlier. Leibowitz succeeded in bringing out the contradictions and errors in her testimony, even though Victoria Price was a determined and stubborn witness who was not easily rattled by his questions.

Leibowitz then presented evidence in court that Miss Price and her friend Ruby Bates were not quite the pure blossoms of southern womanhood that the prosecution had pictured them to be. Instead, they had been prostitutes who for money had bestowed their favors on white and black men alike. Victoria Price had, in fact, been jailed in Huntsville, Alabama, for the crime of adultery.

There was no question in this second trial about whether the Scottsboro nine were receiving adequate counsel. They were, in truth, receiving the best defense available. Leibowitz went after each witness until the story was told straight and understandably; he even showed some witnesses to be outright liars by proving that their "eyewitness" testimony was physically impossible. He methodically chipped away piece by piece at the prosecution's case, but he was saving his blockbuster until the end.

RUBY BATES CHANGES HER MIND

As his last witness for the defense, Leibowitz brought into court the other alleged victim, Ruby Bates.

"Did any rape take place on the Chattanooga-to-Huntsville freight train on the day in question?" he asked.

"No. Not that I know of," was her answer.

When she was asked if there was somehow a possibility that Victoria Price might have been raped, she replied, "No. I was with her the whole time."

Her testimony was indeed startling, but Ruby Bates was not much better on the witness stand than her former friend. Again, there were contradictions, and there were certainly some questions as to whether she had been influenced, or even bribed, to change her testimony. Ruby did not come off as a thoroughly believable witness.

CLOSING ARGUMENTS

After Ruby Bates's testimony, the trial, for all practical purposes, seemed to be over. The case presented to the jury did not appear to come even close to establishing **guilt beyond a reasonable doubt.** Leibowitz was stunned as he listened to a member of the prosecution summing up their case. The lawyer for the prosecution pointed directly at Leibowitz and another lawyer at the defense table but kept his eyes on the jury as he said, "Show them that Alabama justice cannot be bought and sold with Jew money from New York."

Leibowitz objected strongly to such an ethnic slur in the court, but his objection did no good. He realized suddenly and correctly that the case would not be decided on the evidence that had been presented.

The case was finally turned over to the jurors, who after a short while returned their verdict: "Guilty as charged . . . the punishment, death in the electric chair."

ANOTHER SET OF TRIALS

Judge James E. Horton, a man of honor and integrity, was appalled at the verdict. Later, after much thought, he announced that because the jury had reached a verdict so contrary to the evidence in the case, he was throwing out the jury's decision and called for a new trial. It was a brave act and a costly one. Judge Horton was

A political cartoon from the 1930s
about the Scottsboro case. What do
you think it means?

voted out of office shortly afterwards, mainly because of that decision.

The trials went on, now with a new judge who quite clearly was
partial toward the prosecution. At the end of one trial he instructed
the jury on how to reach a "guilty" verdict, but "forgot" to tell them
how to arrive at a "not guilty" verdict. The findings in the new trials
continued to be "guilty" and the sentence death.

ANOTHER ROUND OF APPEALS

Leibowitz appealed the case to the Alabama Supreme Court again.
There he argued that the state of Alabama consistently kept blacks
from sitting as jurors by never placing their names on the lists from
which jury members were drawn. The Alabama Supreme Court,
however, upheld the trial judge, who had found as fact that blacks
were not denied a chance to serve on juries on the basis of their
race.

Leibowitz appealed to the U.S. Supreme Court, which reached
its decision in April 1935. Chief Justice Charles Evans Hughes
pointed out that the Court had previously ruled that state laws ex-

cluding blacks from jury duty denied a black defendant the "equal protection of the laws" as required under the Fourteenth Amendment. Although Alabama law did not exclude blacks from juries, Alabama practices did. That, said the Court's opinion, was unconstitutional also. The Court's ruling helped put an end to this form of discrimination by opening jury service to all citizens. The Court also overturned the verdicts against the Scottsboro nine and ordered new trials to be held.

YET ANOTHER ROUND OF TRIALS AND APPEALS

Back to the Alabama courts they went. Over the next two years, new trials were held, new verdicts of guilty for five of the nine were found, and new appeals were drawn up. More important, however, serious behind-the-scenes bargaining was going on between the defense and the prosecution. Both sides wanted to end this seemingly endless case. Finally, in 1937, more than six years since the time of the alleged crime, charges against four of the defendants—Olen Montgomery, Willie Roberson, Eugene Williams, and Roy Wright—were dropped. The remaining five stayed in jail after they lost their final appeals. A compromise in which Alabama would release the five jailed defendants on **parole** within the next year appeared to be arranged, but the plan was not made public and was never implemented.

It was not until six years later that three of those jailed—Charley Weems, Clarence Norris, and Andrew Wright—were freed. They were refused permission to leave the state, and when Wright did leave, he was put back in jail. Ozie Powell was released in 1946, and in 1948 Haywood Patterson escaped. Finally, in 1950, the last of the Scottsboro nine, Andrew Wright, was released after serving a total of nineteen years in prison.

THE LESSONS OF THE SCOTTSBORO CASES

The Supreme Court had made two important decisions as a result of the Scottsboro trials—one guaranteeing a defendant's right to counsel in a crime punishable by death and the other preventing states from excluding blacks from jury duty because of race. The Court by its actions contributed to saving the lives of the Scottsboro nine, even though it did not keep them from spending many years in jail.

The trials of the Scottsboro nine were a sad commentary on the injustices that can exist within the judicial system. They were a legal disgrace, and they were never justly resolved. It was not until 1976 that the state of Alabama finally made some effort to redress the wrongs done to the Scottsboro nine. In that year, Clarence Norris, the last of the nine known to be still alive, was granted a full pardon by the state, on the grounds that there was proof of his innocence. After receiving the pardon, the sixty-four-year-old Norris told reporters that he felt no malice toward anyone even though "I do feel bad . . . because I was accused wrong." The pardon had come forty-five years too late for this victim of legal injustice.

Testing Your Understanding

1. Who were the Scottsboro nine? What were they accused of doing?

2. What was the immediate danger to the Scottsboro nine after their arrest? Why? How was this danger prevented?

3. Who represented the Scottsboro nine in the first trial? Was this trial fair? Give examples to explain your answer.

4. When their case was first appealed to the U.S. Supreme Court, what legal arguments were made on behalf of the Scottsboro nine? On behalf of the state of Alabama? How did the Court rule on their appeal? What reasons did the Court give for its decision?

5. Who was Samuel Leibowitz? What methods did he use in the second trial? In what ways was he successful? In what ways did he fail?

6. How did Judge Horton rule in the second trial? Why might some persons have considered this to have been a "brave but costly" decision?

7. What argument was raised on behalf of the Scottsboro nine the second time their case was appealed to the U.S. Supreme Court? What had the Alabama Supreme Court ruled? How did the Court rule on their appeal?

8. What did their two appeals to the U.S. Supreme Court accomplish? What was not accomplished?

6
Fred Korematsu

BACKGROUND

In times of war or national emergency, governments often claim extra powers. These powers may temporarily interfere with people's basic rights. When a nation declares martial law, for example, ordinary rights are limited by military rule.

The people who founded this country wanted to avoid giving the military too much power in the government. In the Declaration of Independence, one of the complaints against the king of England was that he ruled the colonies with military force. To maintain military obedience to elected civilian officials, the U.S. Constitution specifically made the president commander-in-chief of the armed forces. Civilian control over the military has since become a measure of democracy.

During both war and peace, our government has always guarded against persons disloyal to this country. In 1798, Congress passed the Alien Acts. Aliens are persons living in the United States who are citizens of another country. These acts allowed the government to deport (that is, send out of the country) aliens who were suspected of being disloyal or dangerous to the young country. The Sedition Act, also passed in 1798, made it a crime for anyone to oppose the federal government. Many people, including future presidents Thomas Jefferson and James Madison, criticized this act for limiting political freedom. Many people believed the Sedition Act would be unconstitutional if used against American citizens. When the Alien and Sedition Acts expired a few years later, they were not renewed.

During the Civil War, President Abraham Lincoln asked Congress to suspend the writ of habeas corpus. This allowed him to arrest and detain civilians suspected of disloyalty. As the Milligan case on pages 1–10 shows, however, the power Congress gave to Lincoln was limited.

During foreign wars, Congress passed laws controlling citizens of enemy countries living in the United States. For example, during the War of 1812, British subjects could not live within forty miles of the eastern coast. In World War I, there was strong anti-German and anti-Italian feeling. German and Italian aliens were allowed to live in this country as long as they acted loyally. Some aliens were arrested and expelled from the country. This happened, however, only if there was evidence showing the person was a danger to public safety.

At the start of World War II, President Franklin D. Roosevelt issued some orders concerning German, Italian, and Japanese aliens. These enemy aliens were forbidden to give information to our enemies or interfere with our defense. It was illegal for them to have guns or cameras. Membership in certain organizations and certain forms of travel were prohibited. The attorney general and the Federal Bureau of Investigation (FBI) arrested enemy aliens who were considered dangerous.

At the same time, the president and Congress made parts of the West Coast a military zone. This was because they feared a Japanese attack. The military commander of that zone first ordered all citizens of Germany, Italy, and Japan to leave the zone. Then he ordered out all persons of Japanese descent. This meant that American citizens were forced to leave their homes because of their race. Since there was no evidence of individual disloyalty by these Japanese-Americans, many people felt they were being discriminated against in violation of the U.S. Constitution.

THE KOREMATSU CASE

In many countries, people have been imprisoned, even executed, without having committed a real crime. In Nazi Germany, being a Jew, a gypsy, or a member of any group considered "undesirable" was reason enough to be sent to a concentration camp or a death chamber. During certain periods in the history of the USSR, Russians whose political ideas were not in line with those of the government were often sent to Siberian labor camps or, according to a common joke, were "lucky" enough to be confined to mental institutions. Even in the United States, as we now remember with regret, human beings were once held in bondage as slaves.

Traditionally, Americans have thought of prisons, reform schools, and juvenile homes as places to confine only those persons lawfully convicted of crimes. Prisoner-of-war camps have been considered places to keep enemy soldiers so that they could no longer fight against American forces. Most citizens of the United States do not like to think that people in this country could be imprisoned or confined because of their political ideas or racial backgrounds, or for any reason other than being found guilty of a crime. The ideal is a noble one, but in cold reality it has not always been upheld. We have only to look at the historical record during World War II to learn this unpleasant truth.

THE NISEI ON THE WEST COAST

When the United States declared war on Japan in 1941 after the attack on Pearl Harbor, approximately 125,000 people of Japanese ancestry lived in this country. Most of them—about 112,000—lived on the West Coast; in this group was a young man named Fred Korematsu, who lived in Oakland, California, with his parents and three brothers. Korematsu was a *nisei* (NEE-say), the term for a Japanese person born in the United States. Just like 70,000 other Japanese-Americans, he was a citizen by birth.

Like many immigrants in the United States, the Japanese lived together in their own neighborhoods or small communities. The older immigrants were reluctant to give up many of their Japanese customs and, for the most part, worked and socialized only among themselves. The American-born nisei, however, did not cling to ancestral tradition. They quickly accepted and were absorbed into the American way of life.

Fred Korematsu's youth was very much like that of any ordinary young American growing up in the peaceful but difficult years before the war. English was his native language, and he went to typical American public schools. He played and followed American sports, hung around with his classmates—Japanese and non-Japanese alike—at a neighborhood drugstore, listened to the same music and radio programs, and dressed in the same style clothes as his non-Japanese friends. Although some people may have had anti-Japanese feelings, Fred Korematsu never had reason to question his rights as an American citizen. These constitutionally guaranteed rights were always there—so he took them for granted. But the Japanese assault on Pearl Harbor on December 7, 1941, changed that with a devastating suddenness.

THE REACTION TO PEARL HARBOR

Not surprisingly, the American people were outraged at the attack and expressed their feelings toward the Japanese nation with bitterness and hatred. For the Japanese-Americans in the United States, a change took place almost overnight. They became "Japs," and were looked on as an extension of the enemy. There was suspicion about their loyalty to America and there was a growing fear that all Japanese were spies or **saboteurs.** The comfortable life that Japanese people had come to know in America became a nightmare. They were denied food and service in stores. Banks refused to release their money or honor their checks. They were insulted and ridiculed in the streets, and some were even attacked and beaten.

Japanese-Americans leave their communities for assembly centers in 1942.

The climax of this attitude came in February 1942, three months after the bombing of Pearl Harbor. The commander of American military defenses on the West Coast, Lieutenant General John L. DeWitt, requested that all 112,000 Japanese-Americans in the area be evacuated and "relocated" somewhere away from the Pacific coast. General DeWitt explained that there was a possibility of a Japanese invasion of the western United States. Because no one really knew which side the Japanese-Americans favored, it was a military necessity to remove them—imperative, the general said, if the United States was to defend its western coast successfully.

Officials in Washington, D.C., at first were skeptical of General DeWitt's proposal. After all, taking a large group of people, most of them American citizens, from their homes and sending them to relocation camps had never been done before in the United States. Moreover, no one was demanding that German-Americans and Italian-Americans be removed from the East Coast, though the United States was also at war with Germany and Italy. It appeared to some that the idea of moving the Japanese was based more on racial factors than on military need. Although General DeWitt had claimed the evacuation was necessary for military reasons, he revealed other feelings in testimony before a Congressional committee when he said, "A Jap's a Jap. It makes no difference whether he's an American or not."

POPULAR SUPPORT FOR THE RELOCATION ORDER

But as the success of the Japanese military actions increased in the days immediately after Pearl Harbor, so did the nation's resentment of the Japanese-Americans. Newspaper and radio reports fueled the fear that the West Coast might be attacked. In Washington, the highly respected columnist Walter Lippmann reflected popular attitudes when he wrote: "I understand fully and appreciate thoroughly the unwillingness of Washington to adopt a policy of mass evacuation and mass internment of all those who are technically enemy aliens. . . . However, the Pacific Coast is officially a combat zone: some part of it may at any moment be a battlefield. Nobody's constitutional rights include the right to reside and do business on a battlefield." The "nobody," of course, referred only to Japanese-Americans.

President Franklin D. Roosevelt issued an order that authorized the Department of War to designate certain parts of the country as

Japanese-Americans line up for inspection at a relocation center in 1942.

war zones "from which any or all persons may be excluded." He persuaded Congress to pass a law that made violation of that order a
crime.

At first, General DeWitt only ordered a curfew for the Japanese-
Americans, which required them to remain in their homes between
8:00 at night and 6:00 in the morning. Later, the Japanese-Americans were asked to relocate voluntarily in inland areas. Only about
7 out of every 100, however, were willing to give up their homes and
jobs. Those who did agree to relocate did not often receive a very
warm welcome in the areas to which they moved. Governor Chase
Clark of Idaho announced, "The Japs live like rats, breed like rats,
and act like rats. I don't want them coming into Idaho. . . ." Newspapers and officials in other states expressed equally harsh feelings.

When most of the Japanese-Americans did not leave the West
Coast voluntarily, General DeWitt issued the final order to move out
all of them. The War Relocation Agency was established hastily to
build camps and supervise all phases of the evacuation as well as
the daily operations within the camps. As soon as the order went
out, the people to be relocated were given forty-eight hours to dis-
pose of their homes and all other property that they could not carry
with them. They were sent to assembly centers for processing and
then to the relocation camps. Living conditions in the camps were

Japanese-Americans weed onions at a relocation center in 1943.

very poor. Workers, some of whom had held good and prosperous jobs before, were paid from $12 per month for unskilled laborers to $19 per month for professionals such as doctors and lawyers. In other parts of the country, German prisoners of war, who had fought against the United States, been captured, and brought to prison camps in the United States, were paid slightly more than $20 per month for their work.

FRED KOREMATSU'S DIFFICULT DECISION

Fred Korematsu decided immediately that he did not want to be interned in a relocation camp. He was twenty-two years old at the time and had a non-Japanese girlfriend whom he did not want to leave. He felt it was unjust and even illegal that he was to be forced into an internment camp. After all, he was a native-born American citizen, and his loyalties were firmly on the side of the United States. He had even tried to enlist in the U.S. Army after the attack on Pearl Harbor but was not accepted.

Because of his strong feelings, Fred Korematsu ignored the re-location order and went into hiding. When confronted by anyone asking about his nationality, he claimed to be Chinese. His pretense did not work, however. Eventually, he was arrested and brought to trial for having violated the evacuation order. The American Civil Liberties Union defended Korematsu in court, but the case was lost. Korematsu received five years **probation** and was sent off to an internment camp at Topaz, Utah.

THE APPEAL TO THE U.S. SUPREME COURT

After this initial defeat, Korematsu's lawyers appealed his case, step by step, all the way to the Supreme Court. Their argument was based on the grounds that it was unconstitutional to take people out of their homes and put them in internment camps solely on the basis of their race. It was noted that other so-called enemy aliens had not been relocated. The lawyers argued that there was no evidence that Korematsu was in any way disloyal. In addition, as an American citizen he had a constitutionally guaranteed right to be treated as an individual and not as a member of a particular racial group.

The lawyers for the government argued that Fred Korematsu and the 112,000 other Japanese-Americans were interned under a lawful military order issued for the protection of America's West Coast. The government lawyers pointed out that it had been proven that certain Japanese-Americans were loyal to Japan and therefore a threat to the war efforts. Because it could not be determined just which Japanese might be disloyal to America, it became a military necessity to remove all Japanese-Americans from a "war zone."

THE COURT'S DECISION

The Supreme Court did not announce its decision until December 18, 1944, more than two and a half years after the original evacuation order. The decision went against Fred Korematsu: six justices upheld the military order, and three voted against it. Justice Hugo L. Black wrote the **majority opinion,** in which he said:

> The military authorities, charged with the primary responsibility of defending our shores, concluded that curfew provided inadequate protection and ordered exclusion. . . . Korematsu was not excluded from the military area because of hostility to him or his race. He was excluded because we were at war with the

The U.S. Supreme Court justices who decided the *Korematsu* case. Justice Hugo L. Black, *first row, second from the right*, wrote the majority opinion; Justice Frank Murphy, *second row, second from the right*, wrote a dissenting opinion.

Japanese Empire, because the properly constituted military authorities feared an invasion of our west coast and felt constrained to take proper security measures. . . .

Disagreeing completely with Justice Black's opinion, Justice Frank Murphy wrote a **dissenting opinion** and referred to the case as an instance of "obvious racial discrimination." Justice Murphy pointed out that loyalty hearings should have been held to determine whether there was cause to remove *individual* Japanese-Americans. Those whose loyalty was doubtful should then be removed. But mass evacuation, he said, was in violation of the constitutional rights to **"due process of law."**

Fred Korematsu lost his case. His conviction was upheld by the Supreme Court despite the strong arguments of Justice Murphy. Perhaps it was because of the times: The United States was still at war with Japan, and the civil rights issues that would find their way to the Supreme Court in the 1960s were not among the major concerns of that day. As for Fred Korematsu, his case was actually being resolved outside the courts, because the War Relocation Agency had already begun a program to do away with the camps and to help the people confined in them to reenter American society. Officials of the agency and other decision-makers in Washington had realized there was really no need for the camps.

Justice Murphy and the other dissenting justices may have been outvoted in the *Korematsu* case, but in their written opinions they left powerful statements about the basic human and civil rights guaranteed by the U.S. Constitution—a guide, perhaps, for later Supreme Courts that would face decisions on the many aspects of civil rights. Justice Murphy said:

> Racial discrimination in any form and in any degree has no justifiable part whatever in our democratic way of life. . . . All residents of this nation are kin in some way by blood or culture to a foreign land. Yet they are primarily and necessarily a part of the new and distinct civilization of the United States. They must accordingly be treated at all times as the heirs of the American experiment and as entitled to all the rights and freedoms guaranteed by the Constitution.

In November 1983, Fred Korematsu appeared before a Federal court, which overturned his 1942 conviction.

Because of the decision in the *Korematsu* case and the fact that the Court has not had occasion to reconsider it, the government still has the power to relocate or intern entire racial groups for reasons of military necessity or national emergency. Let us hope that the situation in which this power would be exercised will never arise again.

Testing Your Understanding

1. Who was General DeWitt? Why did he ask President Roosevelt to declare the West Coast a war zone? Why did he order Japanese-Americans to leave the war zone?

2. Who was Fred Korematsu? Why was he considered a *nisei*? Why was he arrested and tried?

3. Reread the introduction to the case on pages 60–61. What steps had the United States taken in the past to protect against disloyalty by people who were not American citizens?

4. At his trial, what arguments did Korematsu's lawyers use to argue that his arrest was not valid?

5. What arguments did the government use to justify Korematsu's arrest?

6. How did the Supreme Court decide the case? What reasons did it give for its decision? Do you agree or disagree with its decision?

7. What precedent was set in the *Korematsu* case?

8. In 1942, America was also at war with Italy and Germany. Why do you think Japanese-Americans were treated differently from Italian-Americans and German-Americans?

9. Can you think of some other way that the government could have handled the question of possible disloyalty among persons of Japanese descent? Explain your suggested procedure. Would it have been realistic?

70

7

Julius and
Ethel Rosenberg

BACKGROUND

In late 1945, Americans were happy and relieved. The United States and our allies had defeated Germany earlier in the year. Japan, our enemy in the Pacific, surrendered in the face of destruction by the atomic bomb. Now American troops could return home and the nation could devote itself to peace and lead the world to prosperity, or so Americans hoped.

There was not such a happy ending. Instead of finding a "world safe for democracy," the United States found itself confronting the Soviet Union and the threat of communism. Although the "hot" (shooting) war was over, the "cold" war of ideology, the arms race, and the iron curtain had begun. Although fighting on the battlefield had ended, the two nations competed for political allies and international influence.

During the 1920s, however, some Americans had grown to see the Soviet Union as a friend and to sympathize with some of the ideals of communism. The Great Depression of the 1930s had shown some serious flaws in capitalism. During World War II, the Soviet Union was our ally against our enemies and helped us defeat them. Americans had not yet clearly perceived the abuses of Josef Stalin, the Soviet dictator.

Most Americans agreed with their government that communism was an evil and a menace to the world, as well as a threat to capitalism. Communists threatened to use violent revolution to overthrow capitalist governments. Moreover, the communists' claims that they could build a better society appeared false.

To most Americans, the Soviet system was a failure. Government ownership of business and factories and a central, planned economy failed to reach desired goals of increased production and an improved standard of living. Americans pictured people living in Russia and Eastern Europe as unhappy and oppressed by communist dictatorships. On the other hand, most Americans believed that the capitalist free enterprise system provided the greatest good for the greatest number of people.

In order to stop the spread of communism, the United States fought in the Korean War in 1950. American public policy was strongly anti-Soviet and anticommunist. When they were told that American spies had handed over secrets about the atomic bomb to the Russians, Americans felt angered and betrayed. When Ethel and Julius Rosenberg were accused as ringleaders of the spies who stole the secrets, Americans looked at their crime through the lenses of the cold war, the Korean War, and the international communist conspiracy. The spy charges brought home the dreaded realization that America was not secure from foreign attack, nuclear devastation, or internal subversion.

THE ROSENBERG CASE

On the morning of August 6, 1945, an American B-29 bomber approached the Japanese city of Hiroshima. Its bomb-bay doors opened, and a single bomb hurtled down toward the city. The explosion from that one bomb was the mightiest ever made in human history. It destroyed the entire city, killing approximately 100,000 people. The huge mushroom cloud that rose from the ruins of Hiroshima signaled to the entire world that the United States had successfully developed the atomic bomb and that civilization had entered the nuclear age.

The United States now possessed the most powerful weapon in the world. And it was the *only* country in the world that had the atomic bomb. The knowledge of how to make this terrible weapon was the most closely guarded secret in the United States.

THE SECRET BECOMES KNOWN

The secret, however, was not protected well enough. On September 23, 1949, four years after Hiroshima, the Russians exploded their own atomic bomb. Russian spies in the United States had managed

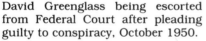

David Greenglass being escorted from Federal Court after pleading guilty to conspiracy, October 1950.

Ruth Greenglass waits outside the courtroom before testifying at the Rosenberg trial.

to obtain secret information on how to construct the bomb. Somewhere in the United States were people who had betrayed their country. At first, no one knew who the traitors might be. But the Federal Bureau of Investigation (FBI) began an investigation, and in 1950 the first arrests were made. In the beginning, several Russian spies were caught. Then, those who had been arrested began telling about others who were involved.

Among those arrested by the FBI was a young machinist named David Greenglass. During World War II, Greenglass had been in the Army, working as foreman of a machine shop at a secret base in Los Alamos, New Mexico. Part of his job was to assemble certain instruments that were to become part of the atomic bomb. He was in a position to learn some of the secrets of constructing the atomic bomb. After questioning, Greenglass admitted that he had given some of these to a Russian agent. But he claimed that he had done so only at the urging of Julius Rosenberg, his sister's husband. As a result of Greenglass's statements, Julius and his wife, Ethel, were arrested. A friend of theirs, Morton Sobell, was also arrested. The Rosenbergs and Sobell were charged with **conspiracy** to commit **espionage.** They could not be charged with **treason** because in the United States the crime of treason is defined as aiding a country with which the nation is at war. And the United States was not at war with Russia.

THE ROSENBERGS
AND THE AMERICAN COMMUNIST PARTY

Julius Rosenberg and Ethel Greenglass were born and raised in a slum neighborhood on New York's lower east side. They grew up in poverty, and their teenage years and early twenties were spent during the hard times of the Great Depression. Julius was able to attend City College of New York, graduating with a degree in electrical engineering. When they met, Ethel was working as a clerk. Partly because of the poverty they had seen and endured throughout their youth, they had both become disillusioned with the capitalist system in the United States. Like many other people in those days, they had joined the American Communist party, hoping that it would offer a solution to the poverty and injustice they saw all around them.

After their marriage in 1939, the Rosenbergs moved into an apartment in a much better neighborhood in the south end of Manhattan. They had two children: Michael (born in 1943) and Robert (born in 1947). Julius Rosenberg worked at various jobs during the 1940s. He had been employed by the U.S. government, but he had been fired as a result of his Communist activities. After holding several other jobs, he went into business with David Greenglass, Ethel's younger brother. Their business had many problems, and it was failing badly at the time of the arrests.

THE EVIDENCE AGAINST THE ROSENBERGS

David Greenglass, the brother and brother-in-law of the accused, was the chief witness in the case against the Rosenbergs. Greenglass had pleaded guilty, and he was waiting to be sentenced on March 6, 1951, when the Rosenbergs were brought to trial.

In his testimony at the trial, Greenglass explained that while he

Separated by an iron grating, Julius and Ethel Rosenberg leave the court in a police van.

was working at Los Alamos, his wife, Ruth, was living in New York. One day, he recalled, Ruth was contacted by Julius Rosenberg, who told her that David was working on the atomic bomb. She was astounded that Julius knew this, because she did not know it herself. According to Greenglass, Julius told her that David could help all humanity by sharing the secret of the bomb with the Russians. First of all, the Russians were our allies, fighting just as hard as we were against the Nazis. Second, it could be disasterous for the world if only one country had the atomic bomb. That country could rule the world. It would be better if two countries had the bomb.

Greenglass claimed that Julius Rosenberg then set up the entire espionage operation. According to his story, Rosenberg had given him half of a torn-up label from a box of Jell-O. He told him that the person who would contact him at Los Alamos to get the secrets would have the other half of the label. This person turned out to be a man named Harry Gold.

Greenglass said that he also gave secret information directly to

Julius Rosenberg. He claimed that while on vacation in New York in September 1945, he sketched the bomb and wrote a description of it. He and his wife Ruth then delivered these to Julius Rosenberg at his home. He said that Ethel typed up the description in the Rosenbergs' living room. This testimony, repeated by Ruth, was the only testimony in the entire trial that directly linked Ethel to the spying activities of Julius.

After the war, David Greenglass left Los Alamos and was honorably discharged from the army. He said that Julius wanted him to continue as a spy, but he refused and returned to live with his wife in New York. The years passed, and it began to seem that his acts of espionage would never be discovered.

THE FBI BREAKS THE SPY RING

In February 1950, a few months after the Russians had exploded their own bomb, it was discovered that one of the English scientists who had worked on the atomic bomb project was actually a Russian spy. His name was Klaus Fuchs. When he was arrested for espionage, Fuchs confessed and named another spy who he said was also deeply involved with the theft of atomic bomb secrets. The name of the other spy was Harry Gold. When Harry Gold was arrested, claimed Greenglass, Julius Rosenberg rushed to him with the news, saying, "It is possible that Gold will mention you. You must leave the country at once."

Greenglass said that he could not go anywhere. His wife had just come from the hospital after having a baby. But Greenglass testified that Rosenberg insisted, giving him $1,000 and outlining a plan for Greenglass and his family to go to Mexico, then to Sweden, from there to Czechoslovakia, and finally to the Soviet Union. Rosenberg told Greenglass to have passport photos taken. Soon, he gave Greenglass an additional $4,000. But before David Greenglass could flee the country, the FBI arrested him.

David Greenglass's testimony was the core of the prosecution's case. It was also confirmed in detail by Greenglass's wife, Ruth, who told almost the exact same story. When the FBI arrested the Rosenbergs, they also arrested the Rosenbergs' friend Morton Sobell. He, too, was charged with espionage and was to be tried at the same time as the Rosenbergs. A prosecution witness named Max Elitcher testified that, according to Rosenberg, Sobell was one of the people who was obtaining military information for him.

76

"For what purpose?" the prosecutor asked.

"To send to the Soviet Union."

Elitcher also claimed that Rosenberg asked him to spy, saying that there were many people who were aiding the Soviet Union by providing them with American military secrets. Elitcher said that Rosenberg had asked him "whether in my capacity at the [Navy] Bureau of Ordinance, working on antiaircraft devices and computer control of firing missiles, would I turn information over to him." The case against Morton Sobell was based on two things: the testimony of Max Elitcher and the fact that Sobell had fled to Mexico, using false names. Sobell had been caught there and returned to stand trial.

JULIUS ROSENBERG TAKES THE STAND

Sobell decided not to take the stand in his own defense. He did not believe that the prosecution had much of a case against him, and he saw no reason to take any chances on the witness stand. The Rosenbergs, however, wanted and needed to tell *their* side of the story. They decided to testify as the key witnesses in their own defense. Julius Rosenberg took the stand first. His lawyer, Emmanuel Bloch, began the questioning.

"What are you being charged with?" Bloch asked.

"Conspiracy to commit espionage to aid a foreign government," Rosenberg answered. Step by step, Bloch asked Rosenberg about the story that David and Ruth Greenglass had told.

"Did you ever have any conversation with Mrs. Ruth Greenglass . . . with respect to getting information from Dave Greenglass out of the place that he was working?"

"I did not," Rosenberg answered firmly.

The questions continued. Did he ever give the Greenglasses money? Did he know of the Los Alamos project? Did he owe allegiance to any other country? Did he tear up the Jell-O box? Did he ask Max Elitcher to obtain information for him? Did he have *any involvement whatsoever* in the espionage activities of his brother-in-law David Greenglass? To each question, Julius Rosenberg gave the same answer: "I did not."

Julius Rosenberg flatly denied every detail of the story that David and Ruth Greenglass had told in court. Furthermore, he said that he and Greenglass had never discussed the subject of spying. Rosenberg said that, just before his arrest, Greenglass demanded that Rosenberg give him several thousand dollars, explaining that he was in trouble and needed the money to get away. When Rosenberg explained that he did not have the money to give him, Greenglass became furious. Now, Rosenberg seemed to be saying that David Greenglass was accusing his own family members in order to obtain a more lenient sentence for himself.

Julius Rosenberg was cross-examined by Irving Saypol, the prosecuting attorney. Throughout the cross-examination, Rosenberg stuck with his story. It was revealed that he had been a communist, but Rosenberg pointed out that this in no way meant he had been spying for Russia.

Ethel Rosenberg was the next witness for the defense. The defense lawyer hoped that the jury would sympathize with her because she was the mother of two young children. Besides she hardly fit the popular image of what a spy should look like. She was pleasant, pretty, and very mild-mannered. Ethel Rosenberg told exactly the same story that her husband had told. She, too, stuck to her story under cross-examination. After a few other witnesses were heard, the case was turned over to the jury. It was up to them to decide who was telling the truth and who was lying. They could either believe David and Ruth Greenglass or Julius and Ethel Rosenberg, but they could not believe both.

THE FINAL ARGUMENTS TO THE JURY

Emmanuel Bloch, the Rosenbergs' lawyer, summed up his case to the jury. He pointed out that David Greenglass was a self-confessed spy, not a person who had always been truthful about his own experiences and beliefs. Besides, there simply was not enough evidence outside of Greenglass's story to convict the Rosenbergs. "We want you to decide this case with your minds, not with your hearts," he said to the jury. "If you do that, you can come to no other conclusion than that these defendants are innocent."

The prosecution, of course, did not agree. The evidence indicated that the Rosenbergs were indeed spies, argued prosecuting attorney Irving Saypol. Furthermore, he said, the Rosenbergs were lying; they were trying to save their own skins. "We ask you to sustain the charge of the grand jury in a verdict of guilty against each of these three defendants, on one basis and one basis alone, the evidence produced in this courtroom as to their guilt of the crime of conspiracy to commit espionage," he concluded.

THE VERDICT AND SENTENCE

The jury retired shortly before 5:00 in the evening, but it was not until 11:00 the next morning that they reached a verdict. The Rosenbergs, Morton Sobell, and the lawyers for both sides were called back into the courtroom. The jury was seated, and the court clerk asked the foreman of the jury if they had agreed on a verdict. "Yes, your honor, we have," the foreman replied. "We the jury find Julius Rosenberg guilty as charged . . . , Ethel Rosenberg guilty as charged . . . , and Morton Sobell guilty as charged."

A week after the jury's verdict, Judge Irving R. Kaufman handed down his decision: a sentence of death for Julius and Ethel Rosenberg. No one else involved in the case received such harsh sentences. Morton Sobell and Harry Gold both received thirty-year sentences, while David Greenglass was sentenced to only fifteen years in prison. His wife, Ruth, was never brought to trial at all.

THE APPEALS

The decision of the judge was a terrible blow to Julius and Ethel Rosenberg; they had not dreamed that their sentence would be so severe. They were scheduled to be executed in May 1951. But there was still some hope: their case would be appealed to higher courts. The courts granted a **stay** while they considered the appeals, and the executions were postponed. The Rosenbergs were not executed in May 1951. After their **reprieve,** their case was appealed again and again. Each time a new appeal was permitted, the executions were postponed again. Their case went all the way to the U.S. Supreme Court.

The appeals on behalf of the Rosenbergs raised many legal issues. First, their lawyers attacked the finding of guilt against the Rosenbergs. They questioned the validity of the Espionage Act, the truthfulness of the Greenglasses' testimony, the fairness of the trial, the correctness of the instructions to the jury, the discovery of new evidence helpful to the Rosenbergs, and many other legal matters. The court of appeals ruled that the Rosenbergs were given a legally correct and fair trial and denied each claim. The conviction was upheld.

At the same time, the Rosenbergs' lawyers questioned the fairness of the death sentence. They argued that the Rosenbergs were basically good people and that the sentences were too harsh, especially in comparison with those of the other spies. The court of appeals ruled that the sentences given by Judge Kaufman were within the law and that it was improper for a court of appeals to change a sentence legally given unless a legal error had occurred.

To reduce the sentences, the court of appeals said, the Rosenbergs could appeal again to the trial judge, Judge Kaufman, or to the Supreme Court. The Rosenbergs' lawyers did so. Judge Kaufman would not change his mind. The Supreme Court voted not to hear the appeal, saying that the important legal issues had already been considered by the court of appeals.

THE WORLD'S REACTION TO THE CASE

The legal battle went on for two full years. During that time, the Rosenbergs were occasionally allowed to see their children in a room at the prison. But for the rest of the time, they were kept in com-

World opinion supported clemency for the Rosenbergs. Here, demonstrators attend a rally in Paris, France.

plete isolation on Death Row. During these two years, the Rosenbergs' case became known throughout the entire world. In Europe, Asia, and the United States, thousands of people signed petitions and marched in protest on the Rosenbergs' behalf. Not all of these people were convinced that the Rosenbergs were innocent. But they objected to their having been convicted almost entirely on the testimony of only two witnesses, David Greenglass and his wife. People felt that this evidence was not nearly enough to justify sending the Rosenbergs to the electric chair. The punishment was simply too harsh.

Many famous people, including Albert Einstein and Pope Pius XII, joined the worldwide protest and wrote to President Dwight D. Eisenhower, asking him to show mercy and clemency for the Rosenbergs. But President Eisenhower would not change his opinion. "The nature of the crime," he wrote, "involves deliberate betrayal of the entire nation and the cause of freedom. . . . The courts have provided every opportunity for the submission of evidence bearing on this case. In the time-honored tradition of American justice, a freely selected jury of their fellow citizens considered the evidence and rendered its judgment. All rights of appeal were exercised and the conviction was upheld. . . . I am determined that it is my duty in the interest of the people of the United States not to set aside this verdict."

ATTITUDES TOWARD COMMUNISM

But more was involved in this case than simply the guilt or innocence of Julius and Ethel Rosenberg. In the early 1950s, the United States and the USSR had become bitter enemies who tried to hurt each other's interests all over the world. In the United States, communism was considered a terrible and dangerous force. Senator Joseph McCarthy of Wisconsin had everyone in the country worried about the communist "menace." He claimed that communist spies were everywhere, in and out of government, and that he was waging a personal crusade against all these enemies of the nation. It was a time of great fear in America, when people were either afraid that the communists were taking over or that they would be accused of being communists themselves. People like the Rosenbergs, who had actually belonged to the Communist party, were hated and feared by millions of Americans. It was in this kind of atmosphere that the Rosenbergs' trial took place.

The Rosenbergs' sons, Michael, *fourth from right,* and Robert, *right,* attend a clemency march in front of the White House.

A FINAL OFFER FROM THE GOVERNMENT

In the end, the government made an offer to the Rosenbergs. If they would *admit* that they were guilty of espionage, the sentence would be reduced to life imprisonment. But the Rosenbergs refused to do this. They said that they had pleaded innocent because they had *been* innocent. They could not admit to committing a crime when they knew in their own hearts and minds that it would not be true. Their execution in the electric chair was scheduled for June 17, 1953. The very day on which it was scheduled to take place, Supreme Court Justice William O. Douglas granted them yet another stay of execution because of a new point of law brought out by their lawyers. But the very next day the full Supreme Court denied the stay, ruling that the point of law would not affect the Rosenbergs' case. Another last minute plea for clemency was made to President Eisenhower. But Eisenhower would not change his decision.

THE EXECUTIONS

Finally, in the early evening of June 19, 1953, Julius Rosenberg, age thirty-five, was executed in the electric chair at New York's Sing Sing Prison. A few minutes later, Ethel Rosenberg, age thirty-seven, was also put to death. The Rosenbergs' deaths did not end their cases. There were too many unanswered questions about their guilt and the harshness of their sentences. As long as people talk about criminal trials, justice, and the death penalty, they will continue to argue the case of Julius and Ethel Rosenberg.

Testing Your Understanding

1. Who were Julius and Ethel Rosenberg? Who were David and Ruth Greenglass? What crimes were they charged with?

2. What evidence was presented against Julius and Ethel Rosenberg at their trial and by whom? What things made that evidence convincing? Unconvincing?

3. What was the verdict of the jury on the Rosenbergs? What was Judge Kaufman's sentence?

4. What issues did the Rosenbergs' lawyers raise on appeal? How did the court of appeals rule?

5. What did the U.S. Supreme Court do about the Rosenberg case? Why?

6. Why did many people protest what was happening to the Rosenbergs?

7. What did President Eisenhower do about the Rosenberg case? What reasons did he give?

8. Compare the punishments received by David Greenglass, Ruth Greenglass, Julius Rosenberg, and Ethel Rosenberg. Do you think these were fair? Explain.

9. Do you think the Rosenbergs would have received a different sentence if they had been tried in 1944? In 1984? Explain.

8
Linda Brown

BACKGROUND

The educational disadvantages American blacks faced at the time of the Brown *case had roots going back to the days when blacks were slaves. The law and practice of slavery kept many blacks from learning to read and write and denied them almost all rights available to free persons.*

Although the Civil War ended slavery, it did not end the common attitudes and economic conditions that went along with slavery. Soon after the slaves were freed, Southern states passed "black codes" that limited Negro rights. These laws were similar to the old slave laws.

To protect the former slaves, Congress and the states approved three amendments to the U.S. Constitution. The Thirteenth Amendment made them citizens and the Fifteenth gave them the right to vote. The Fourteenth Amendment said states could not deny any citizen the "equal protection of the laws."

The traditions of two centuries of slavery died hard. It was difficult for many whites to believe that blacks could be their equals. The system of **segregation** *that started after the Civil War made it hard for blacks to gain equality. When a black challenged segregation in* Plessy v. Ferguson *(1896), he lost. In that case, the Supreme Court said that states could separate blacks from whites traveling in railroad cars as long as both races were given equal facilities. As a result of the* Plessy *case, many states passed laws separating blacks and whites in public facilities such as trains, buses, restaurants, hotels, schools, and even courtrooms. Even where facilities for blacks were worse than those for whites, the federal government did not interfere to make the states provide equal facilities.*

84

Starting during World War I, a large number of black families moved from the farms and fields of the rural South to the factories of southern and northern cities. In the North, they often encountered segregation and racial prejudice similar to what they had known in the South. With World War II, another wave of black families migrated to the North and the West. As demand for workers increased, opportunities for blacks improved. Along with the achievements of blacks in visible fields such as entertainment and sports, and the general economic well-being of many Americans, there appeared to be a change in the nation's attitude toward racial justice.

Some people felt that the lack of educational opportunities for blacks was the major obstacle to racial equality. They believed that equal educational opportunity for blacks was the key to their gaining marketable skills and better-paying jobs. Inferior education for blacks seemed largely the result of segregated public schools. However, in many places, the majority of citizens and elected school officials opposed ending segregation.

The National Association for the Advancement of Colored People (NAACP) led the legal fight to end separate schools for blacks and whites. Their legal argument in the case of Linda Brown was that separate schools could never really be equal.

THE BROWN CASE

Washington, D.C., the nation's capital, is a city filled with monuments honoring great American leaders of the past. In this famous city are kept the originals of the most important documents in American history: the Declaration of Independence and the Constitution, including the Bill of Rights. Washington is also the place where the president of the United States lives and works and where Congress and the Supreme Court meet. The city itself has a reputation as the greatest center of democracy in the world.

In this historic city, on a warm September day in 1950, a small group of adults and youngsters entered one of Washington's junior high schools. The purpose of their visit was to enroll the children in school. But the principal told them that she did not have authority to register *those* children in *that* school. It was a school for whites only, and the youngsters were black.

SEPARATE SCHOOLS

The group then went to the offices of the board of education. There the superintendent of schools told them that the laws of Washington, D.C., required separate schools for blacks and whites. He explained that this was the federal law—created by Congress, no less. Today citizens living in Washington, D.C., can elect their own public officials, who can enact laws with the approval of Congress. At that time, however, laws governing the city were federal laws passed directly by Congress. The superintendent said he could not do anything to help the black children attend an all-white school. Their only hope would be in the courts, which is precisely where the parents then took their case. It became known as the *Spottswood Bolling* case, because that was the name of one of the black youngsters seeking admission to the all-white school.

Ten years after the historic *Brown* decision, Linda Brown and her husband, Charles P. Smith, pose with their son.

Topeka, Kansas, is a small city more than 1,000 miles from Washington, D.C., and, from all outward appearances, very different in many ways. But in Topeka at about the same time, a case similar to that of Spottswood Bolling was taking shape. Linda Brown, an eleven-year-old black girl and the daughter of a minister, wanted to enter an all-white school. The city did not allow her to attend the school closest to her home, which was for white children only. Linda Brown walked past this school on her way to the black school she was assigned to attend. Because Kansas also had a law permitting segregated schools, Linda Brown's request was turned down. Linda's parents decided to go to court and challenge that law.

GOING TO COURT TO CHALLENGE SEGREGATION

Linda Brown and Spottswood Bolling were not the only ones confronting segregated school systems in the early 1950s. In Virginia, South Carolina, and Delaware, three more lawsuits were being started to challenge the segregation of black and white pupils in public schools. The battle that the challengers faced would not be an easy one, because segregated schools had a long history in the United States. From the time when the slaves were freed in 1863, separate schools for blacks and whites were common in the deep South, in the Southwest, and in the border states between the North and South. More than ninety years later, seventeen states, as well as Washington, D.C., still had laws allowing separate schools for black pupils and white pupils. Linda Brown and Spottswood Bolling were only two among 2.5 million blacks and 8 million whites attending segregated schools.

Such schools were able to exist because it was legal at the time to have separate schools *if* they were equal. By providing separate but equal facilities for black and white students, states could claim that they were depriving no one of equal treatment under the Constitution.

The idea of separate but equal facilities was not merely a theory created by states that wanted to maintain segregated schools. It was supported by a U.S. Supreme Court decision made in 1896, more than half a century earlier. The decision resulted from a case called *Plessy* v. *Ferguson.* It involved transportation rather than education, but it laid a foundation for the belief that separate but equal facilities were legal under the U.S. Constitution. Plessy, a black man, was sent to jail in Louisiana for refusing to leave the "whites

As a result of "separate but equal" laws, blacks and whites are forbidden to mix in public schools and other public places.

only" section of a train. The Supreme Court eventually heard the case and ruled that because the railroad provided equal facilities for blacks and whites, the rights of one race were not inferior to those of the other. Therefore, Plessy was wrong. His conviction was upheld, and the practice of segregation for racial reasons was given strong backing.

For more than fifty years after that, a number of states followed the tradition of separate but equal facilities, not only in public transportation and in schools but also in such public places or facilities as stores, theaters, washrooms, and even drinking fountains.

The issue that the lawyers for Linda Brown in Topeka, Kansas, and Spottswood Bolling in Washington, D.C., were taking to court was whether any public school facilities closed off to a person on account of race, no matter how identical in buildings, books, or teachers, were in fact equal. Their lawyers insisted that "separate" was not "equal" and, therefore, was not constitutional. In effect, they were suggesting that the Supreme Court had previously been wrong when it ruled in the *Plessy* v. *Ferguson* case.

Linda Brown lost her case in the District Court of Kansas, and Spottswood Bolling lost his case in Washington. **Plaintiffs** in two similar lawsuits in South Carolina and Virginia also lost. Those four cases were then appealed separately up the judicial ladder to the United States Supreme Court.

In Delaware, however, the fifth case concerning segregated schools was lost by the state. Delaware's supreme court said Delaware's schools for blacks were not in fact equal to its schools for whites. That state's attorney general also appealed the decision to the U.S. Supreme Court, but from the opposite side. And so, in 1952, the Supreme Court agreed to consider all five cases together.

Five teams of lawyers represented the black complainants. Each team was to argue the case for its own client before the Supreme Court. Among the brilliant and respected lawyers representing the plaintiffs was Thurgood Marshall, a black man who had been associated with the National Association for the Advancement of Colored People (NAACP) for many years. During a remarkable career, Marshall was destined to argue more than thirty civil rights cases before the Supreme Court, to be named solicitor general of the United States, and, in 1967, to be appointed by President Lyndon B. Johnson to the Supreme Court, the first of his race to achieve that position.

The arguments on both sides were long and detailed, because the decision that the Supreme Court would make could change the way of life for millions of American citizens, black and white alike. The plaintiffs called for an end to segregated public schools. Segregated schools were unequal, they said, and refusing a person admission to a public school because he or she happened to be black was discrimination. It did not matter whether other equal facilities were available or not. The mere fact that a person was denied admittance to one school only because of race was in itself an act of discrimination and therefore unconstitutional, under the provision of the Fourteenth Amendment to the Constitution. This amendment states that no state shall "deprive any person of life, liberty, or property without due process of law; nor deny to any person within its jurisdiction the equal protection of the laws."

THE CASE FOR THE STATES

On the other side, lawyers for the four states and Washington, D.C., argued that the Supreme Court had already ruled on this issue in the case of *Plessy* v. *Ferguson.* By so doing, the Court had clearly established that separate but equal facilities were constitutionally legal, those lawyers said. In addition, they pointed out that the U.S. Congress—the governmental body that had framed the Fourteenth Amendment—had enacted a law that *required* a segregated school system in the nation's capital. After all, they asked, who could better interpret the meaning of the Fourteenth Amendment than the branch of government that had originally authored it? Congress had in effect interpreted the meaning by enacting a law to permit segregated schools in Washington, D.C., according to this argument.

All five cases dragged on, but in mid-1953 they were interrupted by the death of the chief justice of the Court, Fred M. Vinson. President Dwight D. Eisenhower then appointed a new chief justice, Earl Warren, who in the succeeding years was to become one of the most famous and most controversial members of the Supreme Court.

By the end of 1953, the Court still had not reached a decision in the school segregation cases. Lawyers who had presented their cases were called back for further arguments, and other experts were brought in to add information that the justices felt was essential in reaching their decision.

THE SUPREME COURT ACTS

In early 1954, the Court at last announced that it had made its rulings in those important cases. Two separate decisions would be read. The case involving Spottswood Bolling and Washington, D.C., would be treated separately because it involved only federal law and therefore could not be considered under the Fourteenth Amendment, which concerns state regulations. The other four cases would be ruled on as one. This group of four cases would become known as *Brown* v. *Board of Education of Topeka, Kansas,* only because that particular case headed the list of four as published by the Court.

The *Brown* decision was the first to be read that Monday in 1954. Chief Justice Earl Warren wrote the opinion with the unanimous agreement of all nine justices.

Chief Justice Warren began: "In each of the cases, minors of the Negro race, through their legal representatives, seek the aid of the courts in obtaining admission to the public schools of their community on a nonsegregated basis. . . . The plaintiffs contend that segregated public schools are not 'equal' and cannot be made

The U.S. Supreme Court justices who decided the *Brown* case in 1954. Chief Justice Earl Warren, *first row, third from left,* wrote the opinion.

'equal,' and that hence they are deprived of the equal protection of the laws (*guaranteed by the Fourteenth Amendment*)."

REASONS FOR THE DECISION

The opinion then went on to consider what the authors of the Fourteenth Amendment did intend in regard to racial segregation. The justices concluded that the intentions were unclear. Next, the opinion compared the function and value of education in the year 1954 with the much earlier period when the Fourteenth Amendment was written and found that much had changed. In the 1860s, free public education was just beginning. Education for blacks was almost nonexistent, and practically all former slaves were illiterate because it had been against the law for them to learn to read and write. In modern America, education is important to people's ability to succeed in life and "is the very foundation of good citizenship."

Chief Justice Warren emphasized that everyone was entitled to an equal education. He summed up the findings of the Court briefly but directly: "We come then to the question presented. Does segregation of children in public schools solely on the basis of race, even though the physical facilities and other 'tangible' factors may be equal, deprive the children of the minority group of equal educational opportunities? We believe that it does. . . . Separate educational facilities are inherently unequal."

The Court based its decision in part on evidence that segregation in schools had a harmful psychological effect on black children. It stated that the harm was greater since school segregation had the approval of the law. The Court said that legal separation of the races was seen by both whites and blacks as a sign of blacks' inferiority. And a sense of inferiority could reduce the desires of some children to learn.

The Supreme Court's second ruling of the day, the case of Spottswood Bolling, was in favor of the plaintiffs as well. It was based, however, on the "due process of law" provision of the Fifth Amendment which prohibits unreasonable discrimination by federal laws.

CORRECTING THE PROBLEM

The Supreme Court realized that its school segregation decisions raised enormous difficulties for the states. Schools would have to be integrated on a fair basis. In some cases, new schools would have to be built to replace below-standard schools that black children had been forced to attend. The problems were many. The cases that had just been decided by the Court, Chief Justice Warren pointed out, would remain with the court for further consideration. Having decided the principle of the cases—that public school segregation was unconstitutional—the court wanted to issue a second opinion on how to correct the problem. The Court ordered further briefs and arguments so that it could make recommendations about the ways in which the new ruling should be carried out by the states.

More than a year passed before the Court finished its hearings and made its decision. It told the officials of state and local governments and school boards to end racial segregation in the public schools. The lower courts that first heard cases would keep track of the cases to see that the order was obeyed. To enforce the *Brown* decision, the courts could order school officials to do such things as improve school buildings and assign students to other schools to balance the numbers of blacks and whites more equally.

In this second *Brown* decision, the Supreme Court required the segregating school districts to admit Linda Brown and the other parties to the cases to nonsegregated public schools "with all deliberate speed." Although this directed the school districts to make a prompt start toward ending segregation, it did not set a fixed time limit.

A VARIETY OF SOLUTIONS

The *Brown* decisions put an end to state and local laws requiring separate schools for blacks and whites, but they did not immediately bring about mixing of the two races in many classrooms. Many school systems and courts had their own ideas about the meaning of "deliberate speed." One county closed its public schools for years rather than admit blacks to white schools. Others used pupil placement tests to admit only "qualified" black students. These and other

A police officer escorts black students through a white mob as schools are integrated for the first time in Greensboro, North Carolina, in 1957.

plans appeared to allow equal education, but in practice still resulted in separate schools for blacks and whites.

In many localities, blacks brought lawsuits when illegal segregation was not corrected by the state or locality as the *Brown* opinions had directed. Under *Brown*, local federal district courts were given the power to order the remedies. Where unconstitutional segregation was proven, courts ordered the schools to stop segregating blacks from whites. To balance the number of white and black students in each school of a previously segregated system, courts began to use such methods as requiring certain numbers of blacks and whites in schools and busing students to schools where most students were of a different race.

These solutions were not always popular and are still hotly debated. Despite the Supreme Court's ruling and the lower courts' actions on local lawsuits, ten years after the *Brown* rulings little more than one percent of black school children were attending school with whites in the eleven states of the former Confederacy. When the local lawsuits were appealed to the Supreme Court, the Court again upheld the principles of *Brown*. Fifteen years after *Brown*, when many school districts still resisted and delayed ending unequal educational practices, the Supreme Court said time had run out for compliance with deliberate speed and ordered the end of segregated schools "at once."

DESEGREGATING SCHOOLS IN THE NORTH

It also became clear in the decades following *Brown* that separate schools for whites and blacks was a problem not only in the South but throughout the country. Although there were few "white only" laws on the books in northern cities, blacks and whites in many of these cities often wound up going to different schools. Many school systems kept schools segregated by such methods as busing students to racially similar schools, arranging school attendance zones, and locating schools in single-race neighborhoods instead of between white and black neighborhoods.

As some city school systems desegregated, many white families moved to the suburbs or enrolled their children in private schools. Where extensive "white flight" occurred, the resulting urban school system served mostly black students. To achieve meaningful integration in these urban schools, some people suggested joining the city school districts with the suburban ones. The Supreme Court ruled that courts could not require such "unitary school districts" unless there was proof that suburban or state school officials had done things to contribute to segregation in the city. In other words, courts could not order remedies to racial imbalance in the schools unless government officials had taken illegal actions to cause that segregation. Communities, of course, could always undertake voluntary plans to solve racial inequality in schools.

In addition to the Supreme Court and the lower courts, the next presidents of the United States and Congress worked for school desegregation. President John F. Kennedy introduced the Civil Rights Act in 1963, and President Lyndon B. Johnson saw that it became law following Kennedy's death. Congress also made federal funding available to help school districts reduce segregation and to improve the quality of education for the poor and disadvantaged.

In the 1980s, the issue of separate schools for different races is still a major problem. Although there has been genuine progress in ending segregation in the South, many blacks and Hispanics in the North and West now go to schools where the student body is almost completely made up of minorities.

THE IMPACT BEYOND PUBLIC EDUCATION

Even though the *Brown* decision did not completely end separation of the races in education, it spelled the end to all forms of segregation approved by law. Based on the *Brown* decision, the Supreme

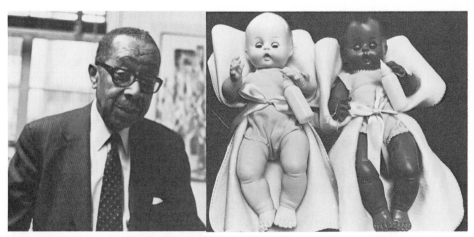

Sociologist Kenneth Clark studied the reactions of segregated children to black and white dolls and found that black children suffered from a definite sense of inferiority. The Supreme Court decision in *Brown* cited Clark's work.

Court and other courts soon said that other kinds of segregation were also unconstitutional. Eventually, for example, public beaches, bus systems, libraries, and parks were open to people of all races.

Linda Brown, Spottswood Bolling, and all the other young people who were part of the school desegregation cases have since grown up. But as youngsters they played a major role in a Supreme Court decision of historic importance. Theirs was a major step forward in the effort to provide equal rights and equal opportunities for all people.

Testing Your Understanding

1. Why did Linda Brown and her parents go to court? How did the lower courts rule in her case before it got to the Supreme Court?

2. What had happened in 1896 in the case of *Plessy* v. *Ferguson*? Why was the *Plessy* case important to the *Brown* case?

3. What other cases were combined with the *Brown* case before it reached the Supreme Court? How were they similar to *Brown*? How were they different from *Brown*?

4. How did the Supreme Court rule in the first *Brown* opinion? What were the main reasons Chief Justice Warren gave for the decision?

5. In its second *Brown* opinion, what did the Court mean when it said that school desegregation should proceed "with all deliberate speed"? How did some states interpret that phrase?

6. What was the legal impact of the *Brown* decision on segregation in areas other than education?

7. In what ways could segregated schools deprive black or white students of equal educational opportunity?

8. Do you know of schools comprised mostly of one race or ethnic group? Should the government take steps to achieve a better racial or ethnic balance in those schools? If so, why, and what steps should they take? If not, why not?

9
Dollree Mapp

BACKGROUND

When the original thirteen colonies decided to join together in one nation, they agreed to a constitution dividing the powers of government between the federal government and the states. For example, the federal government would be responsible for national defense, postal and highway systems, and foreign relations. The states retained the responsibility for the more immediate day-to-day activities of citizens such as marriage and divorce, business enterprise within a state, and the ownership and use of property.

The dual system is also at work in the area of criminal justice. The federal courts try cases involving federal law, while state courts try cases involving state law. Federal criminal laws deal with such matters as treason, mail fraud, and federal tax evasion. The vast majority of crimes are violations of state law and are therefore prosecuted in state courts. For more than 100 years, the operation of the state criminal justice systems was solely within the power of the states themselves.

The Bill of Rights was ratified by the original thirteen states and added to the Constitution in 1791. These ten amendments served as a limit on the power of the federal government. In the 1860s, the Thirteenth, Fourteenth, and Fifteenth Amendments were added, primarily to ensure equal rights of citizenship for the former slaves. An important part of these post-Civil War amendments was the Fourteenth Amendment's due process clause, which required the states to treat persons fairly. Since that time, courts have debated whether the due process clause means that the states must observe the federal Bill of Rights.

The Supreme Court required the states to follow few provisions of the Bill of Rights during the remainder of the nineteenth century. During the twentieth century, however, the Court determined

that most of the provisions of the Bill of Rights were truly "fundamental rights" and therefore essential components of due process.
Gradually, the Court required the states to recognize these fundamental rights. The Mapp case and the Gideon, Miranda, Escobedo,
and Gault cases that follow were each important chapters in the
story of the Supreme Court's effort to apply the Bill of Rights to
state criminal and juvenile justice systems.

Our story begins with the Fourth Amendment and its guarantee of protection from "unreasonable searches and seizures." The
language of the Fourth Amendment, reprinted at the beginning of

A police officer serves a search warrant.

the Mapp *case, describes how police can obtain search warrants and carry out reasonable searches. However, the Fourth Amendment does not say what should happen when an unreasonable search does occur. The Supreme Court did not decide until 1914 on a way to encourage the federal government to use search warrants. It did this by excluding, or keeping out of court, evidence that was found by a search ruled to be unconstitutional. The "exclusionary rule" meant that no evidence seized from a person in violation of the Fourth Amendment could be used in federal court to convict that person of a crime.*

In the 1940s, the Supreme Court decided that the rights in the Fourth Amendment were fundamental rights. The Court required the states to follow the Fourth Amendment. Although it became illegal for state and local police to conduct searches and seizures without a warrant except in a few special situations, states were not required to follow the exclusionary rule. Many people discovered that state and local police could conduct illegal searches and then use the evidence in court to convict them of a crime. This is what Dollree Mapp learned in the late 1950s and what she asked the Supreme Court to change.

THE MAPP CASE

The right of the people to be secure in their persons, houses, papers, and effects, against unreasonable searches and seizures, shall not be violated, and no warrants shall issue, but upon probable cause, supported by oath or affirmation, and particularly describing the place to be searched, and the persons or things to be seized. (Fourth Amendment to the U.S. Constitution)

Privacy is important to Americans. We expect to be free from governmental snooping or spying and to be secure from unwarranted intrusions by the government. These expectations of privacy are protected by the Fourth Amendment to the U.S. Constitution. The Fourth Amendment sets out the right to be free from "unreasonable searches and seizures" and describes how arrest and **search warrants** may be issued.

SEARCHES WITH OR WITHOUT WARRANTS

A search warrant is issued by a judge or other officer of the court, who decides if police have "probable cause" to make the search they request. Probable cause for a search exists when there is a reasonable belief that something illegal is located at a particular place. A reasonable belief may be based on less than certain knowledge, but there must be more information than merely a suspicion or a hunch.

An officer of the court, often called a **magistrate**, must also determine that the warrant describes in some detail what the authorities expect to find and where they expect to find it. The Fourth Amendment encourages the use of warrants so that the government will not first conduct warrantless searches and then justify its action by what it finds.

The words of the Fourth Amendment recognize that, while individuals have a right to privacy, the government has a need to gather information. The police, for example, need to collect evidence against criminals in order to protect society against crime. The amendment considers the interests of both the public and the government.

The Fourth Amendment does not give an absolute right to privacy. It does not prohibit all searches and seizures—only those that are unreasonable. In deciding if a search is reasonable, the courts look at the facts and circumstances of each case. As a general rule, courts usually rule that searches and seizures are unreasonable unless authorized by a valid warrant or justified by special situations. In these special situations, police have a lawful or justifiable reason to discover the evidence. For instance, a person may consent to a search. The evidence, such as a gun on a seat of a car, may be in plain view of the officer. When a lawful arrest is being made, police may search a suspect for their own protection. Also, when an emergency situation arises, such as a bomb threat or house fire, police may find evidence of crime in the course of doing their duty.

DOLLREE MAPP'S ENCOUNTER WITH THE POLICE

When police unreasonably enter a person's house without a warrant, the person may feel helpless to stop them and has good reason to feel angry at them for breaking the law. Dollree Mapp had just that kind of experience. In 1957, she and her fifteen-year-old daughter were living on the second floor of a two-family house in Cleveland, Ohio. Mrs. Mapp was at home alone on the afternoon of May 23 when the doorbell rang. She went downstairs and saw three policemen at the door. One of them told Mrs. Mapp they had reason to believe that someone wanted by the police was hiding in the house.

Mrs. Mapp said she would have to talk to her lawyer before letting the police come in to search. She then phoned the lawyer, who told her: "Ask if they have a search warrant. If they say they do, make them let you see it. It'll be a legal-looking paper that says they are allowed to enter your house and search it. It should be signed by a judge. If they don't have a search warrant, you don't have to let them in."

Mrs. Mapp went back to the door and asked to see a warrant. The policemen looked at each other and then, with more than a trace of irritation, told her that they did not have one. The three policemen trudged back outside and Mrs. Mapp locked the downstairs door. One of the policemen radioed the police station and explained what had happened. Then he joined his two partners in front of the entrance to the house.

The reason the police wanted to search the house was that they had received a tip that a **fugitive** was hiding there. Their **informant** also had told the police that there were gambling materials hidden in Mrs. Mapp's residence.

Mrs. Mapp became steadily more upset as she stared out of her upstairs window, keeping as close a watch on the three policemen as they were keeping on her house. A short while later, a police lieutenant telephoned Mrs. Mapp and told her to let his men come in and search the house. But she repeated what she had told the other policemen and then hung up. The police stayed outside, so Mrs. Mapp called her lawyer again. He told her that she shouldn't worry and that he would come right over. In the meantime, two squad cars pulled up with four more police officers, who got out and joined the three in front of the house.

All seven police officers demanded to be allowed to enter. Mrs. Mapp, talking to them from her second-story window, still refused. A short time later, she saw her lawyer's car pull up in front, and she started downstairs to let him in. She was stopped halfway down, however, by several policemen who had broken into the hallway. Outside, the other police officers stopped the lawyer from entering the house.

"Let me see your warrant," Mrs. Mapp said.

A police officer escorts Dollree Mapp to a police station.

One of the policemen waved a piece of paper in front of her, saying "Don't worry. Here it is." When the officer did not hand the paper to her, Mrs. Mapp snatched it from his hand. The policemen demanded that she give it back, but Mrs. Mapp refused. Then, as the officer tried to grab the paper, she stuffed it down the front of her dress.

"Get that back," one of the other police officers shouted, and grabbed at Mrs. Mapp. She struggled, but he held her firmly while the first officer reached down into the front of her dress and pulled out the sheet of paper. "Now handcuff her," the officer said, as he put the paper into his pocket.

THE HOUSE IS SEARCHED

Several policemen led Mrs. Mapp upstairs to her bedroom where, handcuffed to one of the policemen, she was told to sit on the bed and not to bother anyone. The other policemen then searched her home, room by room. Outside, Mrs. Mapp's lawyer demanded to be let into the house, declaring that what the police were doing was against the law. The officers at first argued with him, but finally just ignored him.

When the entire second floor had been searched and nothing of interest was found, the police went down to the basement of the house. There they opened an old trunk, and inside it found some material—several pamphlets and a few photographs—that the policemen decided were obscene. They took the material as evidence and told Mrs. Mapp she was being placed under arrest for breaking a state law that forbade possession of obscene materials.

Mrs. Mapp protested that the whole thing was ridiculous. In the first place, she claimed, those things did not even belong to her. They were the property of a former tenant who had moved out of the house and had left the trunk and its contents. Mrs. Mapp also said that she and another woman had been planning to send the pamphlets and pictures to their rightful owner. The police informed

The Fourth Amendment to the U.S. Constitution applies to many kinds of searches. Here a narcotics detection dog sniffs a package for drugs at a U.S. Customs station.

Mrs. Mapp that a judge would have to decide on that matter. Their duty was simply to arrest her, not to determine her guilt or innocence. They took her to the police station and charged her with possessing obscene material.

In court Mrs. Mapp pleaded "not guilty" to the charge. During the trial, the prosecution did not produce a search warrant. In fact, there was no testimony that there ever had been a search warrant. But despite the way in which the evidence (the obscene material) was obtained, Mrs. Mapp was found guilty. She was sentenced to serve one to seven years in the Ohio state prison for women.

MRS. MAPP APPEALS

At this point, Mrs. Mapp and her lawyer appealed the case to the Ohio Supreme Court on two grounds: first, the search that discovered the obscene materials was unconstitutional and the evidence should have been excluded at trial; second, the Ohio law prohibiting a person from possessing obscene materials was unconstitutional as well. The court decided by a bare majority of four–to–three that the state obscenity law under which she was convicted was unconstitutional because the way it was written could prevent people from having materials that were not obscene as well as those that were obscene. Such an unclear law violated the freedom of speech protected by the First Amendment of the U.S. Constitution. But there was another problem. According to the Ohio constitution, the state supreme court could not overrule a law if more than one justice voted in favor of keeping it. In Mrs. Mapp's case, three justices had, in fact, voted to uphold the law. Therefore, the state supreme court could not change her conviction even though the majority of four justices thought that it was unconstitutional. The Ohio Supreme Court also decided that evidence obtained by an unlawful search and seizure was admissible in a criminal prosecution in Ohio.

THE QUESTION BEFORE THE U.S. SUPREME COURT

Mrs. Mapp then appealed to the U.S. Supreme Court. In 1961, four years after her conviction, the Court agreed to hear Mrs. Mapp's case. When the case came before the Court, her lawyer did not argue that Mrs. Mapp's rights had been denied by an illegal search and seizure. Instead, he based his case on the argument that the Ohio state law forbidding the possession of obscene materials was unconstitutional—the same point raised by the Ohio Supreme Court. The reason for this approach was simply that the lawyer believed it offered a better chance for a reversal of Mrs. Mapp's conviction. The question of whether the constitutional protections against illegal searches and seizures applied to state court proceedings was a much larger constitutional issue.

Despite the presentation of the case by Mrs. Mapp's lawyer, the Supreme Court decided to rule specifically on the subject of search and seizure. It did so because of the different ways the federal and state governments had been dealing with evidence obtained through illegal searches and seizures. The federal government could not search or seize anything in violation of the Fourth Amendment and, if it did, the evidence it obtained could not be used in court. This was called the "exclusionary rule." States also could not legally authorize their police to conduct searches and seizures in violation of that same amendment. If the state or local police made an illegal search, however, that evidence *could* be used in a state's court. In other words, it was left to the individual states to decide for themselves whether evidence seized by a state's police in violation of the Fourth Amendment could be used to convict a person in state court.

THE COURT'S DECISION

Justice Tom C. Clark wrote the majority opinion for himself and five other justices. After noting that the Fourth Amendment for some time had been enforceable against the states through the due process clause of the Fourteenth Amendment, he announced that "the exclusionary rule is an essential ingredient of the Fourth Amendment" and must also be observed by the states. As a result of this decision, states would no longer be able to use evidence obtained from unconstitutional searches and seizures to get convictions in their courts.

The majority thought that there were no reasons for the Fourth Amendment to be treated differently in federal and state courts. Such a difference could only undermine the protection of privacy that the Constitution provides. Federal law enforcement efforts had not been made ineffective by the exclusionary rule, so neither would those of the states. In fact, many states had begun to adopt the exclusionary rule on their own, since as one state put it, "other remedies have completely failed to secure compliance with the [Fourth Amendment]."

Three justices dissented. They felt that the Court could better have decided the *Mapp* case on obscenity grounds and should at least have had the lawyers re-argue the case to consider the exclusionary rule issue. The real concern of the dissenters was state power, and they felt the Supreme Court should not impose a federal point of view on state criminal matters. In addition, excluding illegally seized evidence could allow criminals to go free because of a police mistake.

The Court ruled that the evidence illegally seized from Mrs. Mapp's home should have been excluded from her trial. Without that evidence, the state had no case against her and dropped the charges. Mrs. Mapp was finally a free person, and the conviction against her was erased from the records. However, the *Mapp* case did not end the debate over the exclusionary rule. Supporters of the decision felt that protecting people's privacy and maintaining their faith in the legal process required the exclusion of illegally obtained evidence. But the opinion's critics argued that public respect for the law would decrease if convincing evidence were excluded from court because of a mistake by the police.

Testing Your Understanding

1. Who was Dollree Mapp? Why did police come to her home in May 1957?

2. How did Mrs. Mapp respond to the police request to search her home? Did she consent to their entry?

3. Should the police have had a warrant to search Mapp's home? What are the arguments for and against them needing a warrant?

4. What crime was Mapp charged with? Where did the police find the evidence? What was the result of the trial?

5. On what grounds did she appeal? How did the Ohio Supreme Court rule?

6. How did the U.S. Supreme Court rule in the *Mapp* case? What reasons did the majority give for their decision? Why did the dissenters disagree with the majority?

7. Assume that an admitted criminal goes free because the police illegally obtained the sole evidence connecting him with a crime and the evidence was not used at his trial because of the exclusionary rule. Should the exclusionary rule be abolished because of situations like this? Explain. Can you think of another way to deal with this problem?

10
Clarence Earl Gideon

BACKGROUND

Do states have to observe the Bill of Rights of the U.S. Constitution? This question has been debated ever since the passage of the Fourteenth Amendment in 1868. The words of that amendment appear to prevent states from interfering with a person's federal constitutional rights. Historically, however, states had been free to make their own laws, which could have differed from federal laws.

The Fourteenth Amendment, for instance, required states to provide "due process of law." Due process refers to the steps in a legal proceeding or trial that protect a person's rights. Initially, the Supreme Court followed the view that a person received due process by whatever legal procedures an individual state chose to provide, so long as they were fair. Gradually, though, the Court decided that due process meant a person was entitled to certain specific, fundamental rights in the Bill of Rights, which all states would have to observe in the same way. Due process, which has been discussed in the Scottsboro trials and the Mapp case, now comes up again.

The Gideon case deals with one of the rights contained in the Sixth Amendment. The Sixth Amendment guarantees a person accused of a crime "the assistance of counsel for his defense," among other rights. Originally, only persons on trial for crimes in federal courts were entitled to lawyers. States were free to conduct their criminal trials in the way they wanted. But in the Scottsboro trial in 1932, the Supreme Court decided that having a lawyer in serious criminal cases was a fundamental right. Therefore, the Court said that the due process clause of the Fourteenth Amend-

ment required states to give free lawyers to poor, uneducated defendants on trial in state courts for crimes punishable by death. This was because poor, uneducated persons would not know enough about the law and the trial process to defend themselves in complicated trials involving the risk of capital punishment. Prosecuting them without providing them with legal help seemed unfair.

After the Scottsboro trials, a number of poor persons accused of less serious crimes in state courts asked for free lawyers. Some states did not give free lawyers to poor persons accused of noncapital crimes. These states told the defendants that they would have to pay for their own lawyers or defend themselves. Some of these defendants appealed to the U.S. Supreme Court, claiming they had a constitutional right to have a lawyer. The Supreme Court ruled, however, that the state courts were not required to provide lawyers free of charge to poor defendants unless there were "special circumstances," or reasons why it would be unfair to force people to defend themselves. Special circumstances included such factors as a case with very complex legal issues or a defendant with a low level of literacy or mental capacity.

When Clarence Earl Gideon, in 1962, asked a Florida judge to appoint a free lawyer to represent him for a "breaking and entering" charge, the judge refused. There were no special circumstances in Gideon's case. He was a person with average intelligence and education who had some experience with the criminal justice system. Although most states provided lawyers to all poor defendants in felony cases, Florida did not. According to the earlier Supreme Court decisions, the U.S. Constitution did not require the judge to appoint a lawyer to represent a person in Gideon's situation.

The Supreme Court took Gideon's case to decide if due process of law should mean that, rich or poor, a person charged with a felony is entitled to a lawyer. If the Supreme Court ruled in Gideon's favor, all states would have to provide lawyers free of charge to poor defendants charged with felonies.

THE GIDEON CASE

In April 1962, Clarence Earl Gideon sat in a Florida state prison writing a letter to the U.S. Supreme Court. He was not an educated man, and he worked hard on the letter, but he knew exactly what

109

he wanted to say. "It makes no difference how old I am or what color I am or what church I belong to if any. The question is I did not get a fair trial. The question is very simple. I requested the court to appoint me [an] attorney and the court refused."

In those few short sentences, Clarence Earl Gideon summed up his problem very clearly, though he did not use the words that lawyers use. Because he could not afford to hire a lawyer, Gideon had asked the court to appoint one for him. The judge had refused, and Gideon went on trial, forced to defend himself on a charge of "breaking and entering."

THE RIGHT TO COUNSEL IN 1962

Gideon knew that the Sixth Amendment to the U.S. Constitution specifically provides that "in all criminal prosecutions, the accused shall enjoy the right . . . to have the assistance of counsel for his defense." But what he failed to understand was that the Sixth Amendment when originally written only guaranteed the *right* to have a lawyer; it did not say that the courts were required to *provide* one for a particular person. In addition, the Sixth Amendment applied only to federal courts; it did not guarantee that right in a *state* proceeding. If, in fact, the right was to be guaranteed in state courts, it would have to fall under the due process clause of the Fourteenth Amendment.

Even so, it seems surprising that in 1962 a person could be put on trial for a crime without the benefit of a lawyer's help. However, it was not an uncommon situation. At that time, the U.S. Constitution only required state courts to appoint lawyers for poor defendants in cases that might lead to the death penalty or cases in which defendants could not adequately defend themselves due to "special circumstances." These circumstances included the seriousness of the crime, the complexity of the defense, and the education and the mental ability of the defendant.

At the time of Gideon's trial, thirty-seven of the fifty states provided lawyers for poor defendants in all felony cases—that is, generally speaking, all those criminal cases in which the punishment could be one year's imprisonment or more. Eight other states *usually* provided lawyers for such cases. The other five states held to the practice of providing lawyers only in capital punishment cases. Unfortunately for Clarence Earl Gideon, Florida was one of those five.

110

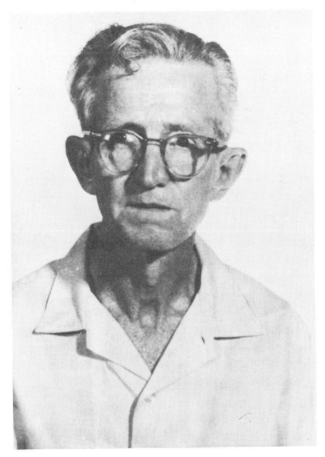

Clarence Earl Gideon

EARLIER SUPREME COURT DECISIONS

The Supreme Court had ruled on this subject several times before 1962. In fact, the Court had ruled on a case very much the same as Gideon's twenty years earlier. The case involved a farmer named Smith Betts who went to trial for robbery in Maryland. He asked the court to provide a lawyer, claiming he could not afford to hire one. The judge turned down the request. Betts appealed to the Supreme Court but he lost his case there as well.

In his prison cell in Florida, however, Clarence Earl Gideon apparently did not know about the *Betts* case. He mistakenly believed that the Constitution required Florida courts to give him a lawyer. Under the *Betts* precedent, Gideon was not entitled to a court-ap-

111

pointed lawyer because he was an average defendant in a case with no "special circumstances." For the Supreme Court to rule in Gideon's favor, it would have to reverse itself and overrule its own precedent, something the Court rarely does.

CLARENCE EARL GIDEON

In 1962, Gideon was fifty-two years old. His wrinkled face and his thin, bent body gave him the appearance of an old man. Life had not been good to him, and he showed it. And the way in which he conducted his life had been less than admirable. He knew that and admitted frankly in a letter about his past, "I will not be proud of this biography . . . ."

Clarence Earl Gideon was born in 1910 in Hannibal, Missouri, a town on the Mississippi River. Gideon's childhood was unhappy. His father had died when Clarence was three years old. His mother was extremely strict, and the boy could not get along at all with his stepfather. So when he was fourteen Clarence ran away, going as far as California. A year later he returned to Missouri but not to his home. Shortly afterwards, he was arrested for stealing clothes from a store. When his mother learned of his arrest, she asked that he be sent to the state reform school. A year later he was released, but his reform school experience was only the beginning of what would become a lifelong series of entrances and exits from various jails.

At eighteen, he was sentenced to ten years in the Missouri state prison for burglary. After three years he was paroled, but in another three years, at the age of twenty-four, he was back in prison, this time at the federal penitentiary in Leavenworth, Kansas, for having burglarized a federal government armory. Three years later, he was outside, again for only three years. Once more Clarence Gideon was arrested in Missouri for burglary and sentenced to ten years. After four years, however, Gideon escaped. He remained free for almost a year, then was recaptured and sent back to the state prison for six more years. That term ended in 1950, but a year later he was in a Texas state prison, serving a one-year term for burglary.

For nine years, from 1952 to 1961, Gideon stayed out of trouble with the law. He married his third wife, and they had two children, both boys. The couple also regained custody of the wife's three children by a previous marriage, and the family moved to Panama City, Florida, a dismal, poverty-ridden town on the northern coast of the Gulf of Mexico.

Gideon's next arrest occurred in an area called Bay Harbor, just outside Panama City. He was charged with breaking and entering a pool hall with the intent of stealing. Ironically, he could have gotten into that pool hall easily because he ran a poker game there for the owner. In court, Gideon staunchly claimed he was innocent and pleaded "not guilty" to the charge.

ON TRIAL WITHOUT COUNSEL

Gideon's trial in Panama City was before Judge Robert L. McCrary and a jury of six people. When he was brought before the bench, the judge asked: "Are you ready to go to trial?"

"I am not ready, your honor," Gideon answered.

"Why aren't you ready?"

"I have no counsel."

"Why do you not have counsel? Did you not know that your case was set for trial today?"

The Supreme Court has ruled that having an attorney is an important aspect of due process in criminal cases. Here a lawyer examines a witness.

Gideon then explained that he wanted the court to appoint a lawyer to help him.

The judge replied: "Mr. Gideon, I am sorry, but I cannot appoint counsel to represent you in this case. Under the laws of the state of Florida, the only time the court can appoint counsel to represent a defendant is when that person is charged with a capital offense. I am sorry, but I will have to deny your request. . . ."

Gideon then had to defend himself. The prosecutor (who was a lawyer, of course) had a key witness, a man named Henry Cook. Cook testified that he had seen Gideon come out of the pool hall in the dark, early morning hours of the day of the break-in.

Gideon cross-examined Henry Cook and called eight witnesses himself. Although Gideon knew something about the law and about trials, he just did not have the skills to ask the right questions to help his defense. At the end of the trial, Gideon addressed the jury and strongly maintained that he was innocent. The jury did not agree and found him guilty. A short while later, Judge McCrary gave Gideon the maximum sentence possible, five years in the state penitentiary.

Clarence Gideon had dropped out of school after the eighth grade, but he was a clever and basically intelligent man. From his many encounters with the law, he had accumulated a fundamental understanding of legal issues, of the individual rights they involved, and of court procedures. It was this knowledge and the indignant feeling that he had been unjustly convicted in the pool hall burglary that prompted him to try to obtain his release from the Florida state prison.

GIDEON'S APPEALS FROM PRISON

First, Gideon filed a **writ of habeas corpus,** a claim that he was being held illegally in prison, with the supreme court of Florida. His writ was based on the argument that he had been denied certain rights because a lawyer was not provided for him at his trial. Florida's highest court, however, rejected that claim.

Gideon then wrote to the U.S. Supreme Court asking for an appeal of the state supreme court's ruling. It would seem unlikely that a poor, uneducated man, in prison after his fifth conviction, would have much chance convincing the Supreme Court to consider his case. But despite his amateur knowledge of the law and the fact that he had access to only a few law books in the prison library, Gideon had filed his request properly and according to the rules set forth by the Court. When the request was received in Washington, it went through the routine channels and finally reached the crucial point at which the court decides whether or not it will review the case.

THE SUPREME COURT
AGREES TO HEAR GIDEON'S CASE

In June 1962, the Supreme Court announced that it would consider Clarence Gideon's case. Gideon had applied for review **in forma pauperis,** that is, as a pauper. Because he was so poor, Gideon claimed, the Supreme Court would have to appoint a lawyer to present his case. The Supreme Court agreed and named Abe Fortas, a senior partner in a highly respected Washington law firm and one of the top lawyers in that city. Fortas was later to be appointed a

Abe Fortas, *above*, argued the *Gideon* case before the Supreme Court in 1962. Three years later, President Lyndon B. Johnson appointed Fortas to the Supreme Court.

justice of the Supreme Court, but in 1962 it was his duty to appear before the Court, and he set about the enormous task of preparing the case for Clarence Earl Gideon.

As he developed his case, Abe Fortas knew that he was asking the Supreme Court to decide that state courts be required to provide lawyers in *all* felony cases where a defendant could not afford one. He was also asking the Court to overrule a decision that an earlier Supreme Court had made on the same subject. In essence, Fortas was asking the justices to admit that an error had been made before.

Fortas built his argument around the fact that it was actually the Fourteenth Amendment to the Constitution that required courts to appoint a lawyer for poor defendants. That amendment provides that *no state* may "deprive any person of life, liberty, or property, without due process of law, nor deny to any person within its **jurisdiction** the equal protection of the laws. . . ." In effect, Fortas pointed out that a person could not get a fair trial without a lawyer and, without a fair trial, any conviction that might result would be without the "due process of law" as guaranteed by the Fourteenth Amendment. In addition, there would not be "equal protection of the laws" for those who could not afford a lawyer and those who could.

Fortas also argued that the decision in the *Betts* case twenty years earlier was a mistake and should be corrected. He asked the Court to reconsider in light of his arguments. By ruling in favor of Gideon, he said, the Court would overturn that decision and thus correct its error.

The lawyers for the state of Florida argued that, first, Gideon was not entitled to a lawyer under the Florida laws and, second, there was no evidence whatsoever that Gideon had not received a fair trial. In any case, the state lawyers argued, the decision to appoint lawyers for the poor in criminal cases should be left up to the individual states.

THE COURT'S DECISION

The Supreme Court found the arguments of Abe Fortas very convincing and reversed the decision in Florida against Clarence Earl Gideon. The Court decided that having a lawyer is "fundamental and essential to a fair trial" and is required by the Fourteenth Amendment to provide "due process of law." By doing so, the Court ensured that in the future no accused person would ever be sent to jail for a felony simply because he or she did not have enough money to hire a lawyer.

Justice Hugo Black, who had been on the Court twenty years earlier and had disagreed with the decision then on the *Betts* case, now was assigned to write the majority opinion in the *Gideon* case. His opinion admitted directly that the Court had been wrong in its earlier judgment. And in 1962, there was no disagreement on the point from any of the other eight Supreme Court justices.

In Florida, Gideon happily received the news that he had won his case and that he would be granted a new trial. At the second trial on the pool hall charge, he had a lawyer who handled his case well. This time the jury found him not guilty.

In the years between the *Betts* and *Gideon* cases, Justice Hugo Black had said, "There can be no equal justice where the kind of trial a man gets depends on the amount of money he has." It had taken a long time, but through the case of Clarence Earl Gideon the ideal expressed by Justice Black finally became more of a reality.

Testing Your Understanding

1. Who was Clarence Earl Gideon? Why was he arrested in Bay Harbor?

2. What did Gideon request from Judge McCrary before his trial? How did the judge respond to his request? What were the reasons for the judge's ruling?

3. What was the result of Gideon's first trial? Do you think he had a fair trial? Why or why not?

4. After being sentenced to prison in Florida, what steps did Gideon take to secure his release?

5. What legal question did Gideon's case present for the Supreme Court? What arguments did Gideon's lawyer make on his behalf? What arguments did the lawyers for the state of Florida make in support of Gideon's conviction?

6. How did the Supreme Court rule in this case? What reasons did it give for its decision? As a result of this decision, were poor defendants entitled to free legal counsel in all criminal cases?

7. Did the Supreme Court's decision set Gideon free? Should it have?

8. In deciding the *Gideon* case, the Supreme Court directly reversed a decision it had made twenty years earlier. Why does the court rarely overrule a precedent? Why might the court change its mind and overrule a previous decision?

11

Danny Escobedo and Ernesto Miranda

BACKGROUND

Earl Warren, who became chief justice of the United States in 1953, was particularly qualified to understand the difficult balance that justice requires. He started his career as the district attorney in Alameda County, California. His office soon had one of the highest conviction rates in the state. He prosecuted criminals vigorously, but he also trained his staff to respect a defendant's right to due process of law. "We don't break the law to enforce the law," he often said. As attorney general of the state of California and, later, as governor of California, he learned firsthand the problems of fairly administering the law. He also came to appreciate the strengths and limitations of state government and the relationship between state and federal government.

The nation soon learned that Earl Warren took seriously his oath of office as chief justice. In it, he swore to administer justice to all people equally. Under his direction, the Supreme Court unanimously decided Brown v. Board of Education, *which said that legal separation of blacks from whites in public education was unconstitutional. In the decisions of the "Warren Court" over the next two decades, individual rights were an important theme. For example,* Baker v. Carr *gave each person's vote equal weight in elections. The* Mapp, Gideon, *and* Gault *cases presented in this book required the states, in addition to the federal government, to observe certain protections guaranteed by the Bill of Rights.*

Many of these decisions caused a storm of protest at the time

Chief Justice Earl Warren

and are still debated today. Some people welcomed what they saw as national standards of justice. Others opposed what they believed was an outside point of view being imposed by the federal government onto the states.

Whatever one concludes about the merits of these issues, it is important to understand one function the Court serves. The Court balances the validity of current law, as an expression of the majority's will, with the interests of those people who are restricted by the laws. The Court decides if the interests denied by law are so essential under the Constitution that they should be treated as rights.

Does the U.S. Constitution require state criminal justice systems to follow certain standards for the prosecution of crimes committed in those states? As in the Scottsboro, Mapp, Gideon, and Gault cases, this was the basic issue in the Escobedo and Miranda cases. In Gideon, the Supreme Court had ruled that the right to counsel and due process of law, which are guaranteed by the U.S. Constitution must be observed by the states in a certain way. If a defendant accused of a felony was too poor to afford a lawyer, states had to offer to provide a lawyer free of charge.

One question left unanswered by Gideon, however, was at what time a person could see his or her lawyer. When the person was officially charged with a crime? Earlier, when the person was first arrested? Or even earlier, when the person was questioned as *a suspect? Also, how were people to know they had this and other rights so they could make use of them? These were the questions the Supreme Court answered in the* Escobedo *and* Miranda *cases.*

THE ESCOBEDO AND MIRANDA CASES

The scene might be any city in the United States. A police officer arrests a suspected lawbreaker. Then, before the suspect can speak, the officer recites some words that sound as if they were memorized: "I must tell you first you have the right to remain silent. If you choose not to remain silent, anything you say or write can and will be used as evidence against you in court. You have the right to consult a lawyer before any questioning, and you have the right to have the lawyer present with you during any questioning. You not only have the right to consult with a lawyer before any questioning,

"Yuh have the right to remain silent. If yuh give up the right to remain silent, anything yuh say can an' will be used against yuh in a court a law. Yuh have the right to an attorney...."

but if you lack the financial ability to retain a lawyer, a lawyer will be appointed to represent you before any questioning, and to be present with you during any questioning."

As this scene suggests, the **interrogation,** or questioning, of a suspect has to follow certain rules and limitations. If a suspect in police custody confesses to the crime, that confession may be presented as evidence in court only if it has been obtained after the individual's rights to an attorney and to remain silent have been explained and are *understood* by the person.

CONFESSIONS THAT ARE NOT VOLUNTARY

Not so long ago, however, such rights were not spelled out. Beating a confession out of someone has always been against the law in the United States, but violence has sometimes been used to coerce a confession. For example, in Mississippi in 1934, deputy sheriffs first threatened to lynch and then severely beat a suspect in a murder. Protesting his innocence, the suspect was released, only to be arrested two days later and severely whipped until he confessed to a statement dictated by the deputies. Two other suspects were also whipped, with a leather strap with a buckle on it, until they agreed to confess as they were told. The three suspects were tried, convicted, and sentenced to death. The only evidence against them was their "confessions." Their appeal eventually reached the U.S. Supreme Court. The Court reversed their convictions, saying that they were denied due process of law and fundamental principles of liberty and justice. A major reason for the ruling was that confessions that are not voluntary—that is, ones that are forced or coerced—are not reliable as evidence.

Besides physical beating, other methods have been used to squeeze confessions out of people. Although less painful, these methods are equally unfair to the person accused. Refusing to let a suspect call a lawyer or any other person until the suspect has signed a confession is a tactic that has been used in many cities, large and small, even though it is illegal. Another method is to frighten suspects by threatening physical beatings or some other consequence so serious that they confess only to save themselves.

Such methods were illegal before the 1960s, just as they are now, because the confessions they produced were not voluntary. But other methods existed that were within the law and were outlined in careful detail in manuals distributed to police departments.

Earl Warren, when he was chief justice of the United States, described these methods and branded them as unfair when he wrote:

> From these . . . interrogation techniques, the setting prescribed by the manuals and observed in practice becomes clear. In essence, it is this: To be alone with the suspect is essential to prevent distraction and to deprive him of any outside support. The aura of confidence in his guilt undermines his will to resist. He merely confirms the preconceived story the police seek to have him describe. Patience and persistence, at times relentless questioning, are employed. To obtain a confession, the interrogator must "patiently maneuver himself or his quarry into a position from which the desired object may be obtained." When normal procedures fail to produce the needed result, the police may resort to deceptive strategems such as giving false legal advice. It is important to keep the subject off balance, for example, by trading on his insecurity about himself or his surroundings. The police then persuade, trick, or cajole him out of exercising his constitutional rights.

On the other hand, Chief Justice Warren recognized that many people confess to crimes of their own free will. There is nothing unconstitutional about a voluntary confession. During their investigations, police may also freely question persons not yet suspects or not under arrest.

In 1964 and 1966, two important cases came before the U.S. Supreme Court that forced police departments throughout the country to change the ways in which they questioned suspects and obtained confessions.

These cases involved two young men, Danny Escobedo and Ernesto Miranda. They were arrested in completely separate cases, but they did have one thing in common: the way each was treated after being arrested.

THE QUESTIONING OF DANNY ESCOBEDO

Danny Escobedo was twenty-two years old and living in Chicago in 1960. In the early hours of January 20, he was arrested and taken to the police station for questioning about the murder of his brother-in-law, which had taken place a few hours earlier. He made no statement to police, and after about fourteen hours his lawyer obtained a release and Escobedo went home.

123

Danny Escobedo

Ten days later, however, police officers arrived at his house again and this time arrested both Escobedo and his sister, the murder victim's wife. They handcuffed Escobedo and led him out to a waiting police car. On the way to the station, one of the police officers told Escobedo that his friend Benedict DiGerlando had said that Escobedo had fired the shots that killed the victim.

"We've got a pretty tight case against you," the police officer added. "For your own good you might as well admit the crime."

"I'm sorry, but I'd like to have advice from my lawyer," Escobedo answered.

After learning of the arrest, Escobedo's lawyer went directly to the police station. There he was told by a police sergeant that his client had been taken to the homicide bureau for questioning.

"I asked Sergeant Pidgeon for permission to speak to my client," the lawyer testified later, "and he [the sergeant] told me I could not see him." Escobedo's lawyer then went directly to the homicide bureau and asked again to speak with his client. Again permission was refused. The lawyer waited for another hour or two, occasionally talking to some of the detectives and continuing to ask to speak with Escobedo. At one point, the lawyer caught a glimpse of his client through an open door and waved. Escobedo waved back and the door was closed quickly. Finally, the lawyer quoted to the police officer in charge a section of the criminal code that gives a lawyer the right to see his client. Then he left to file an official complaint with the Chicago police commissioner.

While all this was going on, Escobedo was only a suspect and had not been charged with any crime. He was questioned but he would not make any statement. Finally, the police brought Di-Gerlando into the room, and the two young men met face to face.

ESCOBEDO'S CONFESSION

"I didn't shoot Manuel, you did it," Escobedo shouted.

Unfortunately for Escobedo, that was an admission that he participated in the crime. Escobedo did not realize that, as a party to the murder, he could be found as legally guilty as the person who pulled the trigger. After a few more hours of questioning, Escobedo said that he had paid DiGerlando $500 to shoot the victim. An assistant state's attorney was brought in, and he carefully wrote down Escobedo's statement, making sure that everything was in a form that would be admissible in court.

At his trial, Danny Escobedo said the confession was untrue and that he had been tricked into making it. Escobedo claimed that the police told him that if he would sign the statement, he would be allowed to go home and would not be prosecuted. The police denied making such an offer. Escobedo's lawyer tried to have the confession thrown out of court, but the judge decided against him. The judge ruled that the confession was voluntary and would be allowed as evidence. Escobedo was convicted and sentenced to life imprisonment.

THE CONVICTION IS APPEALED

His lawyer appealed the case, but the Illinois Supreme Court upheld the original verdict. That court agreed with the trial judge that Escobedo's statements were voluntary. The Illinois court also felt that Escobedo was not entitled to a lawyer until he was formally accused of a crime. An appeal was then made to the U.S. Supreme Court on the grounds that Escobedo had wrongly been denied the right to consult with his lawyer, and that he had not been informed of his right to remain silent.

More than four years after the crime, the Supreme Court passed down its decision: "We granted **certiorari** to consider whether the petitioner's [Escobedo's] statement was constitutionally admissable at his trial. We conclude for the reasons stated below that it was not and accordingly we reverse the judgment of conviction."

THE REASONING OF THE COURT

Justice Arthur Goldberg wrote the majority opinion and explained the reasons for reversing the conviction of Escobedo. Justice Goldberg said Escobedo's lawyer should have been allowed to talk with him as soon as the police took Escobedo into custody as a suspect. Escobedo did not understand the legal impact of some of his statements to the police. If he had been allowed to see his lawyer, he probably would not have made those incriminating statements. In effect, Escobedo had been denied the right to counsel guaranteed by the Sixth Amendment to the U.S. Constitution, a right that was made applicable to state proceedings by the Fourteenth Amendment. Under the precedent established by the *Escobedo* case, a person became entitled to a lawyer when questioned by police as a suspect of a crime.

Several justices dissented. They felt that a person's right to an attorney should only begin after the prosecution formally accuses, or indicts, a defendant. They also believed that the facts showed that Escobedo's confession was voluntary.

The issues of the suspect's right to remain silent and the requirement that the suspect be told that anything he or she did say could be used as evidence in court was not ruled upon at the time. That was to come two years later, in 1966, after the Supreme Court heard the case of Ernesto Miranda.

MIRANDA'S ARREST

About a year before the Supreme Court reached the *Escobedo* decision, Ernesto Miranda was arrested at his home in Phoenix, Arizona, on suspicion of the kidnapping and rape of an eighteen-year-old woman. At the police station, the young woman who had made

126

the complaint said that Miranda was indeed the person who had kidnapped and raped her. Miranda was then taken to a room for questioning. He was not told that he was entitled to have a lawyer present during the questioning, nor was he told clearly that he had the right to remain silent and that anything he did say could be used against him in court.

Miranda realized he was in serious trouble because the police told him that the victim had identified him. Possibly for this reason, he confessed quickly. He explained his version of the crime to the police officers questioning him. A written statement was then drawn up beginning with a paragraph that stated that the confession was a voluntary one, made without threats or promises of immunity from prosecution and made with "full knowledge of my legal rights, understanding any statement I made may be used against me." Miranda signed the confession and was held for trial.

At the trial, Miranda's lawyer objected to allowing that confession to be introduced as evidence, but he was overruled. The jury found Miranda guilty of both kidnapping and rape, and he was given terms of twenty to thirty years imprisonment on each charge. The sentences were to run concurrently (at the same time) rather than one sentence after the other.

THE APPEAL OF MIRANDA'S CONVICTION

The case was then appealed to the Arizona Supreme Court on the grounds that Miranda had not been allowed to talk with a lawyer before being questioned and that during the questioning he had not been truly aware of the consequences of what he said to the police. Miranda claimed he did not realize that what he told the police could be used against him at the trial. Arizona's supreme court ruled against Miranda, noting that in the signed statement Miranda did admit he "understood" that the statement could be used against him. Furthermore, the court said, Miranda had not specifically requested a lawyer and, therefore, the police were not required to provide counsel for him.

Miranda's case reached the U.S. Supreme Court in 1966. In a majority opinion, Chief Justice Earl Warren referred to the Court's decision in the case of Danny Escobedo and pointed out its importance in providing protection for individuals against overzealous police practices. Chief Justice Warren wrote: "The constitutional issue we decide . . . is the admissibility of statements obtained from a

A police officer escorts Ernesto Miranda, *right*, from the courtroom.

defendant questioned while in custody and deprived of his freedom of action."

The case that Chief Justice Warren was writing about was certainly a difficult one. On the one hand, there was the important question of the rights of a person under the protection of the Constitution. On the other hand, there was the equally important issue of interfering with the work of the police and preventing them from arresting criminals and bringing them to trial. Members of the Supreme Court were deeply divided on how the Court should rule.

The smallest possible majority of five justices made the historic ruling: ". . . it is clear that Miranda was not in any way apprised of his right to consult with an attorney and to have one present during the interrogation, nor was his right not to be compelled to incriminate himself effectively protected in any other manner. Without these warnings the statements were inadmissible. The mere fact that he signed a statement which contained a typed-in clause stating that he had 'full knowledge' of his 'legal rights' does not approach the knowing and intelligent waiver required to relinquish constitutional rights."

With those words, the guilty verdict against Ernesto Miranda was reversed. The majority decision spelled out the specific warnings, listed in the first paragraph of this chapter, that police must give before questioning a person in their custody if they want to use the answers as evidence. The majority believed this was the best way to make sure a defendant's statements were made of his or her own free will.

THE *MIRANDA* WARNINGS

Police departments throughout the country from that day forward would have to advise persons in their custody of their right to remain silent and of their right to a lawyer. If police do not give *Miranda* warnings, or continue their questioning after a person has expressed a desire not to talk or has requested a lawyer, no statement can be used as evidence in court.

Police failure to follow *Miranda* procedures does not mean that charges must be dropped and a defendant released. Other evidence besides the unconstitutionally obtained incriminating statements can still be used to convict a defendant. In addition, the arrest may still be valid.

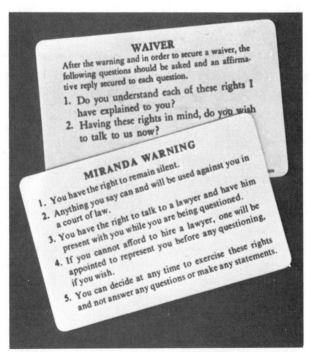

A typical *Miranda* warning card such as the police read to suspects before questioning them.

The dissenters strongly objected to the majority's opinion. They believed that the new rules were not justified by the Constitution or by prior Supreme Court precedent. By making such rules, the Court appeared to be taking on the role of a legislature. They believed that the evils of police questioning were exaggerated. They predicted that the number of confessions would decrease. They also felt that there were other alternatives to the *Miranda* rules, such as having observers in police stations. Finally, they feared that many serious criminals would be set free to commit more crimes.

As a result of the Supreme Court's decisions, the names of Danny Escobedo and Ernesto Miranda became famous. The decisions did not necessarily set them free, however. This was due to the nature of the appeals process. When a court overturns a person's conviction on appeal, the person does not automatically go free. Instead, the person can be given a second trial on the original charge. In the new trial, the prosecution must follow the ruling of the court of appeals.

In Danny Escobedo's case, the Supreme Court had ruled that Escobedo's confession was obtained illegally and could not be used in court. Because the prosecution did not have enough evidence to convict him in a new trial without using his confession, the case against him was dropped, and Escobedo was set free.

The decision of the Supreme Court did not set Ernesto Miranda free, however. Even though Miranda's confession could not be used in court, the prosecution wanted a second trial. In the new trial, Miranda was convicted again, this time on evidence that Miranda admitted his guilt to another person, Mrs. Twila Hoffman. The Supreme Court's ruling did not prevent Mrs. Hoffman from testifying against Miranda because Miranda's statements to Mrs. Hoffman were voluntary and not brought about by illegal police conduct. Miranda was sentenced to twenty to thirty years in the Arizona state prison.

After being paroled, Miranda was arrested again in 1974 for possession of a handgun. Although this final charge was dropped, he was returned to prison for violating his parole. Less than a year later, he was again released. In the spring of 1976, almost ten years after the Supreme Court decision that made his name important in legal history, Ernesto Miranda was stabbed to death in a bar fight. In his pocket were cards with the *Miranda* warning that he had been selling at the local courthouse to support himself. When the police captured one of the suspects in Miranda's killing, they read him his *Miranda* rights.

Testing Your Understanding

1. Why was Danny Escobedo arrested? What did Escobedo do and say while he was in police custody? How did this affect his trial?

2. What arguments did Escobedo's lawyer make when he appealed to the U.S. Supreme Court on Escobedo's behalf? What arguments did the state of Illinois make?

3. What did the Court decide in the *Escobedo* case? Why?

4. What was Ernesto Miranda accused of? What evidence did the police have, and how did they get it? What happened at his trial?

5. On what grounds did Miranda appeal to the Arizona Supreme Court? How did the Arizona Supreme Court rule on these issues?

6. How did the majority of the U.S. Supreme Court rule in the *Miranda* case? Why? How did the dissenters rule? Why?

7. If you had been a justice deciding the *Miranda* case, would you have voted with the majority or the dissenters? Explain.

8. Read again the *Miranda* rights on page 121. From what you know of the *Miranda* decision, answer the following:

   a. Police arrest Joe Adams for theft of a bicycle. When arrested, Adams is riding the stolen bicycle, and the police have two witnesses who saw him steal it. The police take Adams to the station, do not give him any *Miranda* warnings, and ask him where he got the bicycle. Adams confesses. Can the police use the confession against Adams in court? Can Adams get the case thrown out of court for lack of *Miranda* warnings? Explain.

   b. The police, while investigating a murder for which they have no suspects, talk with the victim's family at their home. The police do not give the family members *Miranda* warnings. Can any incriminating statements made by a family member at that time be used against that person in court?

   c. Police ask Mr. O'Brien to come down to the station to "talk about a burglary" and O'Brien comes voluntarily. The police then tell him that he is not under arrest but that his fingerprints were found at

131

the scene of the crime. The police do not give O'Brien *Miranda* warnings. He confesses. Can his confession made without the warnings be used in court?

d. Ms. Drake, a robbery suspect in police custody, is given *Miranda* warnings and says she wants to remain silent. The police stop questioning and leave her alone. Two hours later and still in custody, she calls for the officer and says she changed her mind and wants to confess. After the police tell her the *Miranda* rights again, she confesses. Can the police use that confession in court against her?

9. Assume that a criminal's confession, the sole evidence of his or her crime, was obtained in violation of *Miranda* rights. Is it in the best interests of justice for this person to go free because of an error on the part of law enforcement officials? Explain.

12
Gerald Gault

BACKGROUND

In the United States, juveniles involved with the law are treated differently than adults. This has not always been the case. In the last century, children were jailed with adults, long prison terms and beatings were common, and some children were even sentenced to death for their crimes.

Reformers concerned about the harsh treatment of children urged that a separate court system should be established for juveniles. They believed that children in trouble with the law should be helped rather than punished. Central to the concept of juvenile courts was the principle of parens patriae. *These are Latin words for "parent of the country." The idea is that the government should take care of children and others who cannot legally care for themselves. This meant that the juvenile courts would act as parents or guardians interested in protecting and helping rather than punishing children brought before them. In the reformed system, hearings would be closed to the public; proceedings would be informal; and, if convicted, children would be separated from adult criminals and provided with education and social services to improve their circumstances. Children who broke the law would be viewed as delinquents rather than criminals.*

In 1899, Illinois set up the country's first juvenile court. Today, every state has a separate court system for juveniles. These courts generally handle two different groups of juveniles, the delinquent and the status offender. A delinquent child is one who has committed an act that is a crime under federal, state, or local laws. Status offenders, on the other hand, are youths who are considered unruly or beyond the control of their parents or legal guardians, or who have committed acts that would not be crimes if done by adults. Examples of such acts are violating a curfew, disobey-

ing parents, or being truant from school. Juvenile courts also often have jurisdiction over child abuse and neglect charges.

In most states, a young person charged with a serious crime, such as robbery or murder, can be transferred to criminal court and tried as an adult. These states require a hearing to see if the young person should be transferred. There the court considers the age and record of the juvenile, the seriousness of the crime, and whether the youth can be helped by the treatment offered by the juvenile justice process. As a result of a "get-tough" attitude against juvenile crime, many states in the late 1970s revised their juvenile codes to make it easier to transfer serious or violent offenders to adult court.

In the last twenty years, all states have changed their juvenile justice systems to give children charged with delinquency greater constitutional protections. Courts continue to try to help rather than to punish those young persons. As the Gerald Gault case indicates, however, there was a time in the not-too-distant past when the rights of juveniles were very different from what they are today.

THE GAULT CASE

Gerald Gault was a fifteen-year-old boy who decided one day to make an obscene telephone call. He was sentenced to six years in a state reform school for doing it. Eventually, the case of Gerald Gault was brought before the U.S. Supreme Court, with results that would have a significant influence on the legal rights of young people in the American court system.

Special courts for young offenders had been established long before Gerald Gault was born in 1949. Their purpose was to treat juveniles separately and to keep them out of the system of criminal justice for adults. Before the establishment of such courts, young people in the United States had received the same kind of justice as that allotted to adults. It was not uncommon for children as young as seven years old to be given long prison terms and even death sentences. There is, in fact, a record from the nation's early history of an eight-year-old child who was hanged for the crime of setting a fire.

THE FIRST JUVENILE COURT

As time went on, however, adults began to think that perhaps they were being too harsh with young people who broke certain rules or committed crimes. Judges, lawyers, and thoughtful people everywhere began to consider the idea of treating young lawbreakers differently from adults. Finally, in 1899, the first juvenile court was established in Chicago. Soon after, similar juvenile courts were set up in all the states.

The juvenile courts are quite different from the criminal courts where adults are put on trial. The same kinds of cases may be heard in both courts—everything from littering to murder—but they are handled in very different ways. The idea behind the juvenile court is that it exists to act as a "protective parent" instead of a prosecutor. Its goal is to help and protect young offenders rather than to punish them for crimes that they may not really understand. Since the court acts as a substitute parent, it is responsible not only for delinquent youths but also for dependent and neglected youngsters.

A juvenile case is not a criminal proceeding, no matter what the offense. In an adult criminal case, there is a formal trial with defined court rules. Any particular crime will fall into a specific category, and a set range of punishments exists for each kind of crime. In the juvenile court, each case is treated by itself and is considered

A juvenile court meets informally in the judge's chambers in the early 1900s.

only in terms of the particular person and circumstances involved. The findings of the court are not limited by a specific range of punishments as are adult trials. Instead, the juvenile court's responsibility is to determine in each individual case what care or supervision is necessary or best to help young people overcome habits of delinquency. The idea of a juvenile court is to be just in a legal sense and also to be helpful to the young. But it has not always worked out that way, as Gerald Gault unhappily found out.

GAULT'S PHONE CALL

In 1964, when Gerald Gault was fifteen, his family lived in Gila County, Arizona, a sprawling area of desert, mountains, canyons, and small towns east of Phoenix. One hot, dusty morning in June of that year, Gerald met with a friend, Ronnie Lewis, to decide what to do that day. Their choice was unfortunate.

One of the boys picked up the telephone and dialed the number of Mrs. Ora Cook. When she answered the phone, the boys made some obscene remarks and suggestions. Mrs. Cook listened and then slammed down the phone. One of the voices was quite familiar, she thought. It sounded very much like a neighborhood teenager—Gerald Gault. So she picked up her phone again and called the Gila County sheriff to tell him about her suspicions. Later that morning, the sheriff arrested the two boys and took them to a juvenile detention home.

Gerald's father was out of town on business at the time, and his mother did not get home from work until about six o'clock that evening. When Gerald did not show up for dinner, Mrs. Gault sent his older brother to look for him. He went to Ronnie Lewis's house, where he was told that Gerald was being held at the juvenile home.

DETAINED AT THE JUVENILE HOME

Gerald's brother and his mother went to the juvenile home to find out what had happened. They met with a probation officer named Flagg, who told them about the phone call. He said that Gerald would have to be held at the juvenile home until a hearing the next day in juvenile court.

Gerald, it seems, had an additional problem: he was already on probation. Two years earlier, he and another boy had been involved

136

While he was on probation, Gerald Gault worked in the Job Corps learning automotive and heavy equipment operation.

in a petty theft. Because Gerald had apparently violated his probation, the juvenile officer had sufficient reason to hold him in custody.

After the Gaults left, the probation officer wrote a petition and filed it with the juvenile court. It stated that Gerald Gault was a delinquent minor on probation from the court and asked for a hearing on what should be done about his care and custody. The petition did not mention why Gerald had been arrested that morning. No copy of the document was given to the Gaults.

THE FIRST JUVENILE COURT HEARING

The next day, Gerald, his mother, and his brother appeared in juvenile court before Judge McGhee. Flagg and another juvenile officer also were present. The judge himself questioned Gerald, and after a while the youth admitted that he had dialed the telephone number of Mrs. Ora Cook.

Mrs. Gault was worried. She could see that Gerald's act violated the conditions of his probation, and she realized that her son was definitely in trouble. Yet she hoped the judge would be lenient because the telephone call, although offensive to Mrs. Cook, was

137

hardly a serious crime. As the hearing was coming to a close, Mrs. Gault asked the judge if he was planning to send Gerald to the state industrial school.

"No . . . . I'll think it over," was his answer.

The judge then ended the session, told the Gaults that they would be notified when the next hearing was to take place, and sent Gerald back to the juvenile home. A few days later Gerald was allowed to go to his own home for the weekend. On the same day, his mother received notice that the next hearing would be held the following Monday morning.

THE SECOND HEARING AND THE SENTENCE

At that hearing, Gerald and both his parents appeared before Judge McGhee. The two juvenile officers were present again. Another report had been filed with the court by Officer Flagg, this time charging Gerald with having made lewd and obscene remarks in the presence of a woman. No copy of this report was given to the Gaults, and they did not even know it had been made.

Mrs. Gault requested that Mrs. Cook, the person who had made the complaint, be called to testify. Judge McGhee said that testimony from Mrs. Cook would not be necessary. Then he began the hearing. The judge said he remembered that Gerald had admitted, at the first hearing, to making some of the obscene remarks. The Gaults denied this. They said that Gerald had only confessed to having dialed the telephone number. Officer Flagg said he could not remember, but thought that the Gaults were right. There was no way to find out whose memory was correct, because, following usual juvenile court practice, no records of the previous hearing had been kept.

After more questioning and some additional discussion of what went on at the first hearing, Judge McGhee reached a decision. He ruled Gerald to be delinquent and ordered him confined to the state reform school until he reached twenty-one years of age. If Gerald Gault had been an adult found guilty of the same charge, his sentence might have been a fine of $5 to $50 or a prison term of not more than two months. As a youth, however, he was sentenced to the reform school for a period of six years.

The Gaults felt that this action was neither just nor merciful, but there was little they could do about it. Arizona law did not pro-

A juvenile offender appears before a judge.

vide for appealing juvenile cases to a higher court. Therefore, both the findings of delinquency and the decision to confine Gerald for six years could not be challenged.

THE APPEALS IN ARIZONA

Gerald Gault went off to the Arizona state reformatory. While he was there, however, his parents filed a **writ of habeas corpus,** that is, a petition for a hearing on the legality of confinement. In effect, the writ claimed that Gerald was being held in the reformatory illegally. This was the only way the Gaults could use the law to seek a review of Gerald's case. The writ was referred to a superior court for hearing, but the court apparently felt that Gerald's confinement was legal and dismissed the writ.

The Gaults then appealed this ruling to the state supreme court. Meanwhile, Gerald remained in the reformatory. The Gaults and their lawyer argued for the writ of habeas corpus on the grounds that Gerald had been denied due process of law. They were not asking the court to overrule the juvenile judge's decision about the phone call, but they were claiming that their son had been denied basic and constitutional rights during the juvenile court proceedings. Therefore, the boy was confined illegally and should be released, the Gaults said.

The state supreme court did not share their views, and upheld dismissal of the Gaults' writ of habeas corpus action. This ruling was then appealed to the U.S. Supreme Court. The Court agreed to review the issues of the case; it was only the second time in the history of the United States that the Supreme Court had reviewed a juvenile proceeding.

GAULT'S ARGUMENT TO THE U.S. SUPREME COURT

The Gaults' lawyer based his case on six points in which he claimed Gerald had been denied due process of law. Gerald, he said,

1. had not been granted the right to counsel;
2. had not been informed of his right to remain silent or told that what he said could be used against him;
3. had not been given the right to confront and cross-examine the witness against him;
4. had been denied the right of formal notice of the hearings, the charges, and the possible consequences of his act;
5. had not had the right to appeal his case to a higher court; and
6. had been denied the right to a record of the proceedings against him.

These were rights and protections guaranteed to adults by the Constitution. These rights should have been guaranteed to Gerald Gault, his lawyer claimed, even though Gerald was a minor and his case was in a juvenile court. The lawyer for the state of Arizona disagreed. He argued that because a juvenile court hearing was not a criminal matter, certain rights were not guaranteed. The juvenile court was not prosecuting and punishing the defendant in the way courts would handle an adult case. It was acting as a protective par-

140

ent, prescribing specific treatment for the youth based solely on the circumstances of his individual case.

THE STATE'S RESPONSE

As to specific rights claimed by Gerald Gault, the state's lawyer attacked them one by one:

1. *The right to counsel.* In a juvenile case, parents can employ a lawyer if they desire, but the court was not required to provide a lawyer in the *Gault* case because it was not a criminal proceeding.
2. *The right to remain silent.* Because Gerald's trial was not a criminal trial, this right was not guaranteed. In fact, if the right were provided, the juvenile court judge would be hampered in determining the best "treatment" for the offender.
3. *The right to confront witnesses.* Gerald did not deny the charges against him; he even admitted to some of them. Therefore, there was no reason to cross-examine the woman who made the complaint.
4. *The right of formal notice.* Officer Flagg's informal notice was sufficient because this was not a criminal trial.
5. *The right of appeal.* State law prohibited the appeal of any juvenile case. That was simply the law in existence.
6. *The right to records of the hearings.* Because there was no right of appeal, there was no reason to keep records of the hearings.

The lawyer for the state of Arizona also argued that to grant all these rights would destroy the juvenile court system as it was then set up. For a juvenile court to function properly as a protective parent, the proceedings have to be flexible and informal. Otherwise, the proceedings would be placed back on the level of an adult criminal trial.

THE COURT'S DECISION

The Supreme Court listened to both arguments. Then, on May 15, 1967, almost three years after Gerald Gault's ill-fated telephone call, it handed down its decision. The Court ruled that due process of law as guaranteed by the Fourteenth Amendment to the Constitution applies to juvenile proceedings where a young person is charged with being delinquent. The Court agreed with Gault's lawyers on their first four points and specified the rights that were necessary for a hearing to observe due process:

1. *The right to counsel.* The child and his or her parents must be notified that they have a right to hire a lawyer or, if they cannot afford one, that the court will appoint one.
2. *The right to remain silent.* The constitutional privilege against self-incrimination applies to children as well as adults. Children must be told that they can remain silent and that what they say can be used as evidence against them. *Involuntary admissions* cannot be used as evidence in the hearing.
3. *The right to confront witnesses.* Unless the child voluntarily confesses, a judge cannot rule a child delinquent without sworn testimony by witnesses. The accused person must be given an opportunity to cross-examine these witnesses.
4. *Notice of charges.* The child and his or her parents must be given written notice of the charges or alleged facts in enough time before the hearing to prepare for it.

The Court did not rule on the last two points—a right to appeal and a right to a record of the hearing—because the Supreme Court did not require appeals for all adult convictions. But the Court strongly suggested that juvenile courts should make available an appeals process and a record of hearings to young persons in delinquency proceedings.

Justice Abe Fortas wrote the Court's opinion. He said that the absence of constitutional guarantees deprived some juveniles of fair

A police officer reads the *Miranda* warnings to a juvenile.

hearings and fundamental rights. Justice Fortas noted that "a child gets the worst of both worlds—neither the protections awarded to adults nor the . . . care and rehabilitation (desired) for children." He believed that juvenile courts could observe due process standards without losing the benefits of the separate juvenile justice system. The Court felt that juvenile hearings were similar to criminal trials because they may deny young persons their liberty. Because juvenile courts serve a special protective function, however, they do not have to apply exactly the same due process steps as are guaranteed for adults.

Gerald Gault had finally won his case and had been released from the reformatory. As a result of his experience with the legal system, many of the procedures in a juvenile hearing would be changed. The basic idea of the juvenile court system was not destroyed, as the lawyers of the state of Arizona feared. The juvenile court would still act as a protective parent and not as a prosecutor and punisher of criminals. The changes brought about by the case

143

of Gerald Gault, however, clearly provided certain basic rights and protections that did not exist before. These changes served to strengthen the system, thereby making it more just.

Testing Your Understanding

1. Who was Gerald Gault? What did he do that got him into trouble with the police?

2. What happened to Gault after the police took him to the juvenile detention home?

3. What were some of the differences between the adult criminal justice system and the juvenile justice system that Gault encountered? How do the purposes of each system differ?

4. In what way was Gault's treatment by the Arizona courts fair? In what way was it unfair?

5. What arguments did Gault's lawyer present to the U.S. Supreme Court?

6. How did Arizona defend the operation of its juvenile justice system and its treatment of Gerald Gault before the Supreme Court?

7. What did the Supreme Court decide in this case? What reasons did it give for its decision? Did the Court give juveniles all of the rights that adults have? Explain.

8. In recent years, many states have passed laws that require that juveniles charged with certain serious offenses be tried in adult courts. What are the advantages and disadvantages, to the juvenile and the community, of trying these juveniles as adults?

13
Chicago Eight

BACKGROUND

In the summer of 1968, opponents of the war in Vietnam were determined to make their views known to the delegates of the Democratic National Convention in Chicago. Earlier that summer in Miami, the Republican party had nominated Richard Nixon as its candidate for the presidency. Antiwar activists did not believe that, if elected, Nixon would soon end American military involvement in Southeast Asia. Since President Johnson was not going to seek a second term because of the Vietnam issue, many people hoped for a "peace candidate" to oppose Nixon. Robert F. Kennedy, one promising alternative, had been assassinated earlier in the year.

A number of representatives of different antiwar groups planned protests in Chicago during the convention. The thousands of protesters who came to Chicago probably did not feel they could prevent the nomination of Hubert Humphrey, Johnson's loyal vice president, who had refused to criticize the president's escalation of the war. Although they were not allowed in or near the convention, the protesters wanted very much to make a statement about the war.

The protest organizers asked Chicago city officials for permits to hold meetings and to camp out in Lincoln Park, a large park near the center of Chicago, and to demonstrate near the amphitheater where the convention was held. The city refused to grant the permits and, when the protesters tried to march anyway, the protesters and police clashed. At times the confrontations became violent. Protesters used rocks and bottles and police used dogs, clubs, tear gas, and water hoses.

The violence committed by both the police and the demonstrators shocked people across the country. Newspapers and television *gave more coverage to the marches, demonstrations, and violence outdoors than they gave to the Democrats' convention indoors. A detailed report on the riot later concluded that it was the police, not the protesters, who had rioted. Although some demonstrators provoked the police, the vast majority were peaceful. The police simply overreacted.*

The federal government was greatly upset by the riots and took steps to prevent others from occurring. One step was to charge eight of the police with violating the constitutional rights of the protesters by using excessive force. A second step was to charge eight of the protest organizers and participants with both conspiring to and intending to cause a riot. At issue in both of these trials was the conflict between freedom of speech and the need to protect public order. The police were found not guilty; the trial of the protesters continued for almost six months.

The trial of the protesters, or the Chicago Eight as they became known, was not the usual trial. In fact, it became kind of an angry circus. The defendants and their lawyers showed their lack of respect for the trial by clowning around, criticizing the judge, and continuing their protest of the war in Vietnam. The judge, for his part, openly showed his bias against the defendants.

How could a court of law become an arena for name calling and political arguments by both sides? Perhaps the continuation of the Vietnam War and the failure of the Great Society programs of President Johnson to solve economic and racial problems had something to do with it. Clearly, Americans were questioning national goals and national leadership. Should we really be surprised that the rules of law were also questioned?

THE CHICAGO EIGHT CASE

The year 1968 was a time of great turmoil in the United States. In that year, the number of Americans on combat duty in Vietnam reached nearly 550,000. Thousands would die or be injured during that bloody year, fighting in a war that many Americans had come to disapprove of. In the United States, many young people took to the streets to protest American involvement in Vietnam. Some burned their draft cards and refused to go into the armed forces. Others moved to Canada to avoid being drafted. As the year went on, the protests became stronger. It was becoming clear that a majority of the American people opposed the Vietnam War.

The blame for American military involvement was laid squarely on President Lyndon B. Johnson. It was he who had raised the number of military personnel in Vietnam from 20,000 to 550,000. The feeling against the war and against Johnson's administration was so strong that in the spring of 1968, Johnson went on television and told the people of the United States that he would not run again for president that fall.

A YEAR OF VIOLENCE, A YEAR OF PROTEST

The year 1968 was also one of violence in the United States. James Earl Ray shot and killed Dr. Martin Luther King in Memphis, and Sirhan Sirhan assassinated Senator Robert F. Kennedy in Los Angeles. Even the protests and demonstrations against the war in Vietnam were becoming violent. This time of conflict and domestic strife reached a climax in August 1968 at the Democratic National

Chicago police and demonstrators clash during the 1968 Democratic National Convention.

147

Convention in Chicago. There the Democratic party would choose its candidates for president and vice president.

Various protest groups throughout the United States decided to go to Chicago during the convention to stage demonstrations. Thousands of people began arriving from all parts of the country. Most of them were in their late teens and early twenties, but there were many middle-aged and even elderly people as well. Among them were college professors, laborers, students, and school dropouts. They had all come to have their say about the war in Vietnam. But Chicago was not prepared to give them a warm welcome. The city of Chicago was run almost entirely by the Democratic party machine, presided over by Mayor Richard J. Daley. In addition to being mayor, Daley was also a very powerful figure in national politics. Once, when John F. Kennedy was still a senator, he was asked what he would do first if he wanted to run for president. "I'd call Mayor Daley in Chicago," he answered. The last thing Mayor Daley wanted was a lot of protest demonstrations that might spoil what Daley thought of as "his" city and "his" convention. But the demonstrators came anyway.

PROTESTERS AND POLICE CLASH

They gathered in Lincoln Park, a sprawling area on Chicago's lakefront that contains a zoo, large grassy spaces, and sports facilities. They planned to camp there at night and use the park as a base from which to stage their protest marches. But Mayor Daley had other ideas. They were refused an official permit to gather at the park, and they were ordered to leave the area. When they would not leave the park, the Chicago police moved in and tried to force the demonstrators out. Still the protesters would not move. At that point, the police waded into the crowd of more than 3,000 demonstrators with billy clubs and tear gas. In the battle that ensued, many protesters were injured. Others fled into the streets and the police followed in pursuit.

That night, there was violence all over Chicago, on the part of both the police and the protesters. The demonstrators accused the police of brutality, and the police accused the protesters of violent and illegal acts. News of the police attack and the riots spread quickly throughout the United States. Other people left for Chicago to join the protest. Soon, as many as 20,000 protesters had gathered in Chicago.

Mayor Daley and the police announced that they would "hold the line" against the demonstrations. The protesters grew angry and began to taunt the police. The police attacked again, and the riots began once more. The situation became so bad that the National Guard was called out. People throughout the country saw news pictures of police clubbing demonstrators or carting them off in police vans. Hundreds of demonstrators were injured, or arrested, or both. Many police officers were hurt in the rioting as well.

THE CHICAGO EIGHT

Among the protesters were eight men, some of whom were leaders of various radical groups; the others were prominent leaders of antiwar rallies. The eight were Jerry Rubin and Abbie Hoffman, co-founders of the Youth International Party (better known as the Yippies); Rennie Davis and Tom Hayden, two of the founders of Students for a Democratic Society (SDS); David Dellinger, the only middle-aged member of the group, a well-known pacifist and opponent of the Vietnam War; Bobby Seale, head of the Black Panther party; Lee Weiner, a sociology instructor at Northwestern Univer-

The Chicago Seven hold a press conference. They are, *left to right*, Abbie Hoffman, John Froines, Lee Weiner, David Dellinger, Rennie Davis, and Tom Hayden. Seated in front are Jerry Rubin and Nancy Kurshan. She was not involved in the trial.

149

sity; and John Froines, a chemistry instructor at the University of Oregon. Before long, they would become known throughout the nation as the *Chicago Eight.*

The rioting in Chicago and the Democratic convention finally ended, and the protesters went back to the cities and towns they had come from. But the federal government wanted to prevent such disturbances from happening again. Ramsey Clark, attorney general under President Johnson, thought about prosecuting the leaders of the demonstrations for violating an antiriot law recently passed by Congress. He did not do so because his staff of lawyers decided that the antiriot law might be unconstitutional, and because investigations showed that it might have been the police rather than the demonstrators who actually caused the riot.

THE DECISION TO PROSECUTE

In November 1968, the Republican candidate Richard Nixon was elected president, defeating the Democrat, Hubert Humphrey. Not long after taking office in January of the next year, the Nixon administration reviewed former Attorney General Clark's decision and decided to prosecute the Chicago Eight for violating the antiriot law. The Nixon administration believed the antiriot law was constitutional and that there was evidence that the Chicago Eight had violated the law. The relatively new law was designed to prevent "outside agitators" from going from state to state starting riots. However, the law had not yet been tested in court.

The antiriot law made it a crime to travel from one state to another "with intent to incite, ... organize, promote, encourage, participate in, or carry on a riot . . . ." Such conduct could be made a federal crime because the federal government has the power to deal with things having to do with more than one state, such as business, communication, or travel among different states. State law, not federal law, is the usual way to deal with riots that happen within a state.

There were two major ways that the antiriot law could possibly violate the U.S. Constitution. The first has to do with the idea that the law punishes a person's *intent* rather than what the person actually does. A person who wanted to start a riot could be convicted of "intent to incite a riot," even if no riot ever took place. In addition, proof of a crime of intent requires a look into the mind of the accused person. A basic principle of a free society, however, is that a person can be punished for actions, but not for thoughts. A law punishing a person's intent to cause a riot comes dangerously close to crossing that line.

The second reason the antiriot law might be unconstitutional is that it might punish people for saying things they have a right to say. What people say is usually protected by the First Amendment's freedom of speech clause. To protect freedom of speech, the government cannot punish a person for violent words unless those words are both spoken to cause lawless action and likely to cause lawless action. For example, assume a person says to a peaceful crowd, "This government is no good. We should do something about it." The First Amendment would probably prevent a person from being punished for those words. On the other hand, assume a person says to an angry crowd with torches and gasoline cans, "This government is bad. Let's burn down city hall right now." The government could charge that person with a crime because the First Amendment does not protect that kind of speech. The reason for the distinction is that in a free society people should be able to complain about the government, but should not be allowed to endanger lives and property in doing so. The antiriot law may have permitted punishment of speech that should have been protected by the First Amendment.

The Nixon administration also charged the Chicago Eight with another crime. The second crime was **conspiracy** to travel from one state to another with intent to incite a riot. Under the law, conspiracy is two or more persons planning and doing at least one step toward committing a crime. The conspiracy charge is a separate crime from the crime being planned. For example, if three people plan to rob a bank and then rob the bank, they can be charged with both conspiracy to rob a bank and bank robbery. Also, if three people plan to rob a bank and buy the car to be used for the getaway, they can be charged with the crime of conspiracy to rob a bank, even if the bank robbery never takes place.

The American Civil Liberties Union (ACLU) called the trial of the Chicago Eight "probably the most important political trial in the history of the United States." It was called a "political" trial because many people felt the government was punishing the Chicago Eight for their opposition to the Vietnam War, their attempts to make their views known to the American people, and for their different lifestyles as much as for intending to cause a riot. Many people felt that it was unfair to try to punish people for something they did not actually do or cause. In fact, investigations showed that the riots may have been caused by police efforts to break up what had originally been peaceful demonstrations.

THE ISSUES AT STAKE

The questions at issue in this trial concerned the basic freedoms guaranteed by the Constitution. Where did the right of free speech, the right to assemble, and the right to protest end and a threat to public order and safety begin? The people of the United States were deeply divided over these questions. Many even opposed bringing the eight to trial in the first place. But many others strongly favored it. The trial of the Chicago Eight was destined to become one of the wildest and most controversial trials ever held in the United States.

The trial itself began on September 24, 1969. Federal District Court Judge Julius J. Hoffman was appointed to preside in the case. He was stern and politically conservative, the kind of judge who would accept nothing but the strictest obedience and respect.

The prosecuting attorney was Thomas Foran, U.S. attorney for the state of Illinois. There were several defense lawyers, led by William Kunstler and Leonard Weinglass. The site for the trial was the Federal Court Building in downtown Chicago. The authorities feared that large protest demonstrations would be held and, even worse, that more rioting would break out. Therefore, armed guards were placed at the entrances of the Federal Court Building. Visitors were turned away unless they could show that they had some legitimate business there. Purses and briefcases were searched for hidden weapons.

DIFFICULTIES WITH JUDGE HOFFMAN

From the very beginning of the trial, there was a serious problem between Judge Hoffman and the defense lawyers. When four of the defense lawyers resigned from the case, they sent a telegram to the judge to inform him of their decision. But Judge Hoffman considered this highly improper. He was furious that the lawyers had not resigned *in person,* and he had them brought to Chicago. When they arrived, he charged them with contempt of court and had two of them put in jail. Many lawyers from all over the country protested against Judge Hoffman's action. The judge eventually reversed his

Judge Julius Hoffman

decision and released the defense lawyers from the charge of contempt.

Next, Charles Garry, the lawyer that Bobby Seale had hired was unable to come to Chicago at that time because he was about to enter the hospital for an operation. Garry was noted for his experience and success in defending political dissenters. Seale asked that his own trial be postponed until the lawyer of his choice was able to defend him. Judge Hoffman turned down Seale's request. Then Seale requested permission to defend himself, claiming that it was his constitutional privilege to do so. But Judge Hoffman refused to allow this and decided instead that the chief defense attorneys, Kunstler and Weinglass, could defend him. Seale protested, saying that he did not want them to represent him, and he dismissed them from his case. Judge Hoffman said he could not do that. Seale called the judge a "racist." Judge Hoffman replied that Seale could be held in contempt of court for remarks like that.

THE PROSECUTION'S CASE

The prosecution opened the trial by explaining that it intended to prove that the eight defendants had, first, conspired to cross state lines for the purpose of starting a riot and, second, had actually travelled across state lines with the intention of causing a riot. The prosecution then pointed out each of the defendants by name to the jury. They were all wearing black arm bands as symbols of their protest against the war. When his name was called, Tom Hayden held up his fist in the Black Power salute. The judge warned him against doing that again. Abbie Hoffman chose a different way to greet the jury when he was introduced. He blew them a kiss. At that point, Judge Hoffman instructed the jury "to disregard the kiss thrown by the defendant Hoffman."

According to the prosecution, the intent-to-incite-to-riot charge had three distinct aspects:

1. Before coming to Chicago, the defendants had intended to cause violent protests.
2. They had planned and organized for many people to come to Chicago to protest against the war in Vietnam.
3. Once the demonstrators and the Chicago Eight were in Chicago, the Chicago Eight had urged the protesters to riot, and the protesters were willing and ready to do so.

To prove the conspiracy charge, the prosecution had to show that the defendants met together and agreed on a plan to cause a riot and actually took steps to put that plan into action.

The defense lawyers pointed out that the First Amendment to the U.S. Constitution guaranteed freedom of speech, of the press, and of the right of people to assemble and to petition the government for a redress of grievances. They argued that the defendants were simply exercising their rights under this constitutional protection. In order to convict the Chicago Eight, the defense argued, the prosecution would have to prove that the defendants had intended to start a riot and had this intent before coming to Chicago and had *participated in* or *caused* a riot once they were in Chicago.

COURTROOM ANTICS

The prosecution began by taking testimony from certain police officers and from witnesses from Mayor Daley's office. But the main case for the prosecution was based on the testimony of certain "police informants." These were spies who had infiltrated the protesters' groups to report on their activities to the police. When the informants began to testify, however, the trial began to get out of hand. After one "spy" witness had testified, Bobby Seale arose and requested permission to cross-examine the witness. Judge Hoffman refused his request, saying that he already had a lawyer (Kunstler) to do that for him. "That man is not my lawyer," Seale said, and he continued to try cross-examining the witness.

Judge Hoffman admonished him saying that he would hold Seale in contempt of court if he continued to ask the witness questions. "I admonish *you!*" Seale shouted in reply. "You are in contempt of the people's constitutional rights." Then another defendant, Tom Hayden, shouted, "Let the record show that the judge was laughing."

"Yes, he is laughing," Seale added.

At that point, Judge Hoffman sent the jury from the courtroom. The argument between the judge and Bobby Seale continued while the jury was absent. Seale continued to demand his right to defend himself, and he refused to listen to the judge. Judge Hoffman finally said: "I am warning you that the court has the right to gag you. I don't want to do that. But under the law you may be gagged and chained to your chair." Judge Hoffman then recessed the court. But when he asked all in the courtroom to rise, Bobby Seale and the other seven defendants refused.

On another occasion, seven defendants tried to bring a birthday cake into the court to present to Bobby Seale. The judge refused to allow them to do it. "Hey Bobby, they arrested your cake," one of the defendants yelled, as a federal marshal took the cake away from Jerry Rubin. "Cakenapping!" another one cried. The incident ended there, but it was a vivid example of the way the trial was going.

As other witnesses appeared, Seale repeated his demands to be given the right to question them. At one point he called the judge a "fascist" and a "pig." After this outburst, Bobby Seale was gagged and handcuffed to a chair in the courtroom. This was something that had never been done before in a major trial in the United States. It was indeed a strange and terrible sight to see in an American courtroom. And it did not really make things easier. Seale could still mumble and disrupt the court with his demands to defend himself. Finally, Judge Hoffman declared a **mistrial** in the case of Bobby Seale, found him in contempt of court, and sentenced him to four years in prison. It was believed to be the longest sentence for contempt of court ever given in the history of American justice.

A drawing depicting Bobby Seale after Judge Hoffman had ordered him to be bound and gagged during the Chicago Eight trial.

THE APPEAL OF SEALE'S SENTENCE FOR CONTEMPT

While the prosecution of the other defendants continued, Seale appealed Judge Hoffman's contempt citation and long sentence. The higher court eventually ruled in Seale's favor. The court of appeals said that Judge Hoffman could have cited Seale for contempt as he did, but that Seale should then have received a separate trial for contempt by another judge to determine whether the contempt citation was justified and, if so, what the sentence should be. Given the circumstances, there was too great a possibility that the actual trial judge, Judge Hoffman, might have been prejudiced against Seale and therefore unable to make a fair determination of punishment for contempt. The government decided not to bring Seale into court again and dropped the contempt charges. The government dismissed the original conspiracy and intent to riot charges as well.

The Chicago Eight had suddenly become the Chicago Seven. The other defendants, outraged at Judge Hoffman's treatment of Bobby Seale, began to follow his example. They, too, spoke out in court strongly and with as little restraint as Seale. Judge Hoffman contributed to this difficult situation. He began to shout back at the defendants and to ridicule them. He did other irritating things, such as deliberately mispronouncing the name of defense attorney Weinglass, calling him "Weinruss" or some other similar name. Meanwhile, the prosecution proceeded with its case. A total of fifty-three witnesses testified that the defendants did attend the protests, that they did urge people to participate in protest marches, that some of them did give speeches at the protest, that some were beaten, and that all were arrested during the chaos. But it was not clear that the witnesses for the prosecution had proved that the defendants had planned and actually caused the Chicago riots.

THE DEFENDANTS' CASE

The defense produced a varied and interesting assortment of witnesses. There were college professors, radicals, famous writers (such as Allen Ginsberg, Norman Mailer, and William Styron), folksingers, a state senator (Julian Bond), a former attorney general of the United States (Ramsey Clark), and even Chicago's mayor (Richard J. Daley). The defense was basically more of a broad expression of political ideas and beliefs than an attempt to show that the defendants were innocent. The defense believed that the defendants' guilt had not been proven at all. In their view, the constitutional right of free speech, the freedom to assemble and protest, and the evil of the war in Vietnam were all too important to omit from the trial. They considered these to be the fundamental issues of the entire case.

The trial dragged on for weeks. Witness after witness took the stand, and the trial became increasingly wild. Defendants (and sometimes even spectators in the courtroom) called Judge Hoffman names such as "tyrant," "liar," "a disgrace to the Jews," "Hitler," and "Julie." At one point, David Dellinger had his bail revoked and was sent to jail for his interruptions in the courtroom. The defense lawyers and Judge Hoffman exchanged bitter words throughout the trial. It was clear that there was little good will or even respect between them. Judge Hoffman constantly ruled *against* all motions

157

by the defense and *for* all those made by the prosecution. He even argued with the defendants and their attorneys, often shouting loudly at them. At one point, defense attorney Kuntsler referred to Judge Hoffman's court as "a torture chamber."

On February 10, 1970, the trial finally approached its end, as both the prosecution and the defense summed up their cases for the jury. The defense condemned the use of police spies, arguing that the main purpose of the trial was to shift the blame for the riots from the Chicago police to the protest organizers. The entire trial was political, the defense lawyers said, and should have been thrown out of court in the first place. The prosecution charged that the defendants willfully misled innocent young people and incited them to riot. Furthermore, the prosecution said, the seven defendants had conspired together to cause the riots that had erupted in Chicago.

CONTEMPT CHARGES AND JURY VERDICTS

On February 14, the jury retired to discuss the case and reach a verdict. As soon as the jurors had left the courtroom, Judge Hoffman announced that he was holding the seven defendants and their two lawyers in contempt of court and that he would now sentence them for the things they had done during the trial. He read each count of contempt against the defendants. Then, he read the sentences. David Dellinger received 29 months, 13 days; Jerry Rubin: 25 months, 23 days; Rennie Davis: 25 months, 14 days; Tom Hayden: 14 months, 14 days; Abbie Hoffman: 8 months, 6 days; John Froines: 5 months, 15 days; and Lee Weiner: 2 months, 8 days. The judge saved the largest sentence for lawyer William Kunstler. He was charged with 24 separate counts of contempt and sentenced to 4 years and 13 days in prison, longer than the sentence given earlier to Bobby Seale. Leonard Weinglass received a sentence of 20 months, 9 days.

The defendants were denied bail by Judge Hoffman and taken off to jail. The jury deliberated for several days. Finally, it looked like there would be a hung jury (a jury that cannot reach a verdict). In cases where the jury cannot agree, a mistrial is usually declared. On the day that the motion for a mistrial was to be presented, however, the jury announced that they had reached a decision.

The court was called into session. The jury found the Chicago Seven *not guilty* of conspiracy. Froines and Weiner were found not guilty of the other charges, but the remaining five were found guilty of crossing state lines to incite a riot. Judge Julius Hoffman sentenced Dellinger, Davis, Hayden, Rubin, and Hoffman to five years in prison and a fine of $5,000. This was the maximum sentence the judge could give under the law. One of America's strangest and most "political" trials was finally over, after almost five months.

THE APPEALS

The case of the Chicago Seven did not end with the judge's sentences, however. The Chicago Seven appealed their convictions, their contempt citations, and their failure to be released on bail. The lawyers appealed their contempt citations.

Attorney William Kunstler talks with reporters after he was sentenced for contempt.

Approximately one week after the trial, a higher court reversed Judge Hoffman's decision not to allow the defendants to be free on bail. The defendants were then released while the other appeals were made to higher courts.

First, the five defendants who were found guilty under the antiriot law appealed their convictions. The court of appeals ruled that the antiriot law did not violate the Constitution, but granted the five a new trial on other grounds. The appeals court found that Judge Hoffman had made several legal errors in selecting the jury and in keeping out of court certain evidence that may have been favorable to the defendants. The appeals court also found that Judge Hoffman had such a negative attitude toward the defendants that they did not get a fair trial. The government decided not to bring the defendants to trial another time on the antiriot law charges and dropped the charges against the defendants. That meant that Dellinger, Davis, Hayden, Hoffman, and Rubin were freed from their convictions and sentences of five years in jail. But they, Froines, Weiner, and their lawyers still faced jail terms for the contempt citations.

Second, the court of appeals considered the appeals of the Chicago Seven and their lawyers to overturn the contempt citations for their courtroom behavior. The appeals court ruled that the trial judge, Judge Hoffman, could legally cite them for contempt, but that they were entitled to a trial on those charges before a judge other than Judge Hoffman in order to make sure that the judge was not unfairly prejudiced against them. The appeals court also overturned some of the contempt citations against Kuntsler and Weinglass.

This time, the government brought the Chicago Seven to trial on the contempt charges before a new judge. Judge Edward Gignoux heard the four-and-a-half-week trial in 1972, four years after the original trial. Judge Gignoux found Froines, Weiner, Davis, Hayden, and Weinglass not guilty of the contempt charges, and these people were at last free of all charges stemming from the Chicago riots and the first trial. Judge Gignoux found Kunstler, Dellinger, Rubin, and Abbie Hoffman guilty of some of the contempt charges against them but suspended their sentences. The new judge felt that the defendants and their attorneys had broken court rules, but that their poor behavior in the courtroom was largely provoked by Judge Hoffman.

The trial of the Chicago Eight has left many questions unanswered. Should the protest leaders have been brought to trial in the first place? Should the defendants and their lawyers have behaved the way they did in court? Were they justified in their actions because the trial was highly political? Should Judge Hoffman have acted as he did? Should he have allowed the trial to become so undignified? Should there have been a mistrial? The questions go on and on.

The Vietnam War is now over, and so is the trial of the Chicago Eight. But the controversy surrounding both of these events will remain alive for many years to come.

Testing Your Understanding

1. Who were the Chicago Eight? Why did they come to Chicago in 1968?

2. Where did the protesters want to go in Chicago? Did the city of Chicago give them permission? What did the police do?

3. What crimes were the Chicago Eight charged with? What did the government have to prove in order for the Eight to be convicted?

4. Why was the trial called a "political trial"? How did the Chicago Eight behave during the trial? Why do you think they acted the way they did?

5. Who was the judge in the trial? How did he conduct the trial? Do you think he was fair to the defendants and their attorneys? Explain your answer.

6. How did the Chicago Eight become known as the Chicago Seven?

7. After the trial, the judge cited the Chicago Seven and their attorneys for contempt of court and sentenced them to jail for long terms. Did they have to serve these sentences? Explain why or why not.

8. What did the jury decide in this case? What was the final result of the charges? Explain.

9. If you had been the mayor of Chicago during the 1968 Democratic National Convention, how would you have handled the thousands of people who came to the city to protest?

14

Lieutenant William L. Calley

BACKGROUND

After defeating the fascist forces of Germany, Japan, and Italy in World War II, the United States turned toward protecting the world against communism. Many Americans feared that communism would take over Asian governments by armed force. China and North Korea were already communist countries. The "cold war" became a "hot war" when North Korean soldiers invaded South Korea in 1950. Although the communists were defeated in Korea, they threatened other nearby countries. According to the domino theory, Asian countries were lined up like a row of dominoes. If the communists knocked one over, the rest would follow.

Many Americans viewed Vietnam as a key domino in danger of communist takeover. The communists had already beaten the French there in 1954. That caused Vietnam to be divided into communist North Vietnam and noncommunist South Vietnam. Americans wanted South Vietnam to be a proving ground for democracy in Asia. South Vietnam, however, became a dictatorship. Communists in South Vietnam began to make terrorist attacks against officials, teachers, nurses, and doctors. The South Vietnamese government killed people suspected of being communists. The brutality of both sides generally created a feeling that there was no law in South Vietnam, only violence.

In 1960, North Vietnam started sending groups of armed South Vietnamese exiles into South Vietnam. The exiles were men who had gone to the North when Vietnam was divided. To help the South Vietnamese government, the United States sent military advisers to train its army. As the North Vietnamese sent more armed forces into the South and more of South Vietnam came un-

der communist control, the United States sent more American soldiers. Soon, the American soldiers were fighting in direct combat against the communists in Vietnam. Although Congress never declared war, it did approve American involvement. At the beginning of 1969, the peak of American involvement, 542,000 American soldiers were in Vietnam.

South Vietnamese civilians were in the middle of the fighting in many places. The communist forces would take their food, hide in their villages, and sometimes pretend to be innocent civilians. The American troops distrusted the Vietnamese civilians in combat zones because it was hard to tell friends from enemies. In communist-controlled areas, the American soldiers would sometimes declare "free fire" zones, where anyone who moved would be shot. Civilians were warned to leave these areas, but often they had nowhere else to go. They slept in family tunnels next to

American soldiers in Vietnam often had to fight in rugged terrain where ambushes were not uncommon.

their huts at night and worked in their fields and villages during the day.

Fighting was difficult and dangerous for Americans in South Vietnam. Almost all combat took place in the rugged countryside: fields of wet rice paddies and grass taller than one's head, dense jungle forests, and rocky, wooded mountains. The Vietcong, as the communist forces were called, usually hid during the day and attacked at night. The enemy hid in tunnels to avoid American bombs and cannon fire and often ambushed Americans when they least expected it.

Lieutenant William L. Calley and his platoon had experienced those dangers firsthand. A month before its attack on the suspected communist village of My Lai, the platoon had taken heavy losses when it became trapped in a mined field. Although Calley himself was on leave that day, he helped the helicopters unload the wounded and dead. As they watched their friends being killed by booby traps, mines, and enemies they could not see, the American soldiers were angry at an enemy they could not find and fearful of the constant risk of death. Calley and his men expected the worst when they entered the village of My Lai.

THE CALLEY CASE

The dreadful story of My Lai started on the morning of March 16, 1968, when American artillery shells began to explode among the scattered grass shacks and small buildings that made up this tiny South Vietnamese village. After the bombardment stopped, U.S. Army helicopters appeared in the sky and then landed quickly in a nearby field. A company of American soldiers scrambled out and, crouching, raced out from under the whirling helicopter blades. The soldiers had expected to face fierce armed resistance from the Vietcong, but instead they found nothing but silence. No one shot at them, and no Vietcong could be seen anywhere. The soldiers moved quickly toward the village of My Lai.

THE LIEUTENANT IN CHARGE

Commanding the first platoon of soldiers was Lieutenant William L. Calley, a quiet, baby-faced young man who was nicknamed "Rusty" because of his light red hair. As a result of the things that happened

Lieutenant William Calley, Jr.

in My Lai that morning, Lieutenant Calley would later stand accused of the mass murder of more than 100 people.

When he entered the village of My Lai in 1968, William Calley had been in the army for almost two years. Before entering military service, he had tried his hand at many things. Calley had never been a good student. He had graduated from high school almost at the bottom of his class and had then flunked out of junior college. Later, Calley took a number of jobs, ranging from railroad conductor to private investigator, but he did not keep any of his jobs for very long.

Finally, late in 1966, William Calley enlisted in the army and decided to become an army officer. He began his training at officer candidates' school in Fort Benning, Georgia, in March 1967. The school and military training were rugged, and they lasted throughout a seemingly endless spring and summer. When the training period was over, Calley graduated near the bottom of his class. U.S. military involvement in Vietnam was very intense and expanding rapidly at that time, and there was a definite need for new second lieutenants to serve in combat operations. Calley was given his second lieutenant's bars and assigned to the 11th Light Infantry Brigade in Hawaii. From there, Calley soon went into combat in Vietnam. On March 16, 1968, Lieutenant William L. Calley, twenty-four years old, led his platoon in an attack on the village of My Lai.

THE MISSION AT MY LAI

Many stories would later be told about what happened in My Lai on that terrible morning, and each story was different from the next. One fact, however, stood out among all the conflicting accounts, a fact disputed by no one. This was that, in spite of the fact that no armed resistance had occurred, almost all the people of My Lai were dead by noon of that day. No one knows exactly how many victims there were, but it has been estimated that more than 400 Vietnamese died in My Lai. All the buildings, houses, and grass shacks in the village had been burned to the ground. All the animals had been killed.

A report of the mission at My Lai was later written at command headquarters by Lieutenant Colonel Frank A. Barker, and it told quite a different story. "Upon landing," Colonel Barker said in his report, "the rifle companies assault[ed] enemy positions, making a detailed search of all buildings, bunkers, and tunnels." As a result, the report continued, 128 Vietcong had been killed in action and 11 had been captured. But surprisingly the only enemy equipment reported captured or taken from all those "Vietcong"—aside from canteens, medical supplies, and so forth—were three rifles, made in the United States. Perhaps to explain why there were no civilians left alive in My Lai after the battle, Colonel Barker ended his report with the following words: ". . . the civilian population supporting the Vietcong in the area numbered approximately 200. This created a problem in population control and medical care [for] those civilians caught in the fire of the opposing forces. However, the infantry unit on the ground and helicopters were able to assist civilians in leaving the area and in caring for and/or evacuating the wounded."

But the My Lai mission had not happened that way at all. Later, the truth would be revealed, and it would shock the entire world. For the moment, however, the My Lai massacre was quickly covered up and conveniently forgotten.

RONALD RIDENHOUR'S CHARGES

The war in Vietnam went on. Lieutenant Calley remained in command of his platoon, and he was even promoted to the rank of first lieutenant. His unit continued to fight in Vietnam, conducting assaults on the Vietcong, search-and-destroy missions, ambushes, patrols, and all the other dangerous business of war. When Calley's tour of duty in Vietnam ended, he volunteered to stay for an additional year and was reassigned to a company of Army Rangers. By then, My Lai had become a thing of the past, and no one really thought much about it anymore. No one, that is, except a soldier named Ronald Ridenhour.

Ridenhour himself had not taken part in the My Lai mission, but he had heard rumors about it, and these rumors aroused his curiosity. He began to ask questions, and the answers he received from some of the men who *had* been there all pointed to one conclusion: some terrible **war crimes** had been committed at My Lai. Ridenhour gathered as many details as he could, and, when his period of military service was over, he wrote to the army, to the Department of Defense, and to members of Congress, telling them everything he knew about what had occurred at My Lai.

THE ARMY INVESTIGATES

The army decided to begin investigating Ridenhour's charges. In June 1969, Lieutenant William L. Calley received orders to report back to Washington, D.C., in connection with an army investigation of the incidents at My Lai. When he arrived in Washington, army officers questioned Calley and told him that there was a possibility he might be charged with murder. He was then sent to Fort Benning, Georgia, to await the outcome of the investigation. On September 4, just two days before he was scheduled to be discharged from the army, charges were finally filed against Lieutenant William Calley. A formal hearing was scheduled to be held in the office of the judge advocate general at Fort Benning.

The results of the army investigation soon became known to the public. The story was out in the open now: all the details of the bloody slaughter of women, children, and old people. The outcome of the investigation affected not only those who were present at My Lai but also those who had tried afterwards to cover up the truth. These included several colonels and even the commanding officer of the entire division, Major General Frank Koster. But the central figure in the investigation was Lieutenant William Calley; the massacre had occurred as a result of his actions and the direct orders he had given to others. On November 24, 1969, Calley was formally charged with murder in the first degree. In all, he was accused of having murdered *at least* 102 Vietnamese civilians at My Lai, including women, children, an old priest, and a two-year-old baby.

THE COURT-MARTIAL BEGINS

The general **court-martial** at which Calley would stand trial for murder was set to begin on November 17, 1970. The court-martial board would be composed of six officers who ranged in rank from colonel down to captain. The law member, who would serve as judge, was Colonel Reid Kennedy, a career army lawyer. Calley's chief defense attorney was an experienced civilian lawyer by the name of George Latimer, a specialist in military law. The prosecution was to be led by Captain Aubrey Daniel, who was serving as an army lawyer after having been drafted. Captain Daniel was twenty-eight years old at the time. It seemed strange that the army placed the prosecution of such a tremendously important case in the hands of such a young and inexperienced lawyer. But Aubrey Daniel would prove his worth as an attorney.

In his opening remarks to the court-martial board, Daniel described the story of My Lai in brutal detail. When Calley and his platoon arrived at the village, Aubrey Daniel explained, they found only old men, women, and children, none of them armed. There was no hostile fire. There was no combat. Daniel then told the whole horrible story of how Calley had simply executed unarmed Vietnamese civilians.

When he concluded his opening remarks, Daniel called Ronald Haeberle to testify as one of his first witnesses. Haeberle had not only been at My Lai, but he had also taken photographs there. Some of the photographs showed U.S. soldiers, and others showed a large pile of dead bodies in an irrigation ditch, the bodies of some of the Vietnamese who had been killed at My Lai that day. Daniel then called on a number of soldiers who had been involved in the mission but who had not been in Lieutenant Calley's platoon. The soldiers testified that there had been no resistance that day from the Vietcong, that there had been many dead civilians at the scene, and that Ronald Haeberle's photos had been taken of those same dead

168

Major Kenneth Raby, *left*, one of Calley's defense attorneys, and Captain Aubrey M. Daniel, *right*, the prosecutor in the *Calley* case, visit My Lai to investigate the alleged massacre.

civilians. In all, about twenty witnesses testified to seeing dozens of dead civilians.

The next person to testify was an army helicopter pilot named Hugh Thompson, who had seen the shooting of the Vietnamese civilians, as well as the piles of dead bodies, as he was flying over My Lai. Thompson said that he had immediately landed to demand that Calley stop the slaughter, but that Calley had refused. Thompson then took some of the wounded onto his helicopter and flew them out of My Lai. In all, he made three rescue flights that morning.

Up to that point in the trial, Captain Daniel had been merely laying the groundwork for the prosecution by establishing that certain war crimes had been committed at My Lai. Now he proceeded to the next phase, that of establishing that Lieutenant William Calley had committed those crimes. He began by calling the former members of Calley's platoon to the witness stand.

Robert Maples, a former machine gunner in Calley's platoon, spoke to the jury: "Calley was there at the ditch [where the pile of dead bodies had been photographed]. They had people standing by the hole. Calley and [Private First Class Paul] Meadlo were firing at the people. They were firing into the hole. . . .[Calley] asked me to use my machine gun . . . [but] I refused." A number of other soldiers placed Calley at the scene of the ditch, talking with the helicopter pilot and firing shots into the ditch.

Meadlo himself was to be the next witness, but he refused to testify. Although he had been released from the army, he was still afraid of what might happen to him for his part in the My Lai massacre. Colonel Kennedy offered to grant Meadlo **immunity** if he testified; this meant that he could never be prosecuted for any of his testimony in Calley's trial. But Meadlo still refused to talk, and he was turned over to the military police.

The next witness to take the stand was Private Dennis Conti. According to Conti's testimony, Lieutenant Calley had instructed him to round up about six women and children who were nearby. "I brought them back to Calley on the trail. There were others there—thirty or forty. All were women and children. I remember one old man. . . ."

"Who was with them?" prosecutor Daniel asked.

"The only G.I. I remember was Meadlo."

"What happened then?"

"Calley told me and Meadlo to take the people off and push them in a rice paddy. We took them out there, pushed them off the trail, and made them squat down and bunch up so they couldn't get up and run. . . ."

"What was Meadlo doing at this time?"

"He was guarding the people," Conti answered.

Daniel asked him what happened after that.

"Lieutenant Calley came out, and said, 'Take care of these people.' So we said, 'okay,' and we stood there and watched them. [Calley] went away, and then he came back and said, 'I thought I told you to take care of these people.' We said, 'We are!' 'No,' he said, 'I mean kill them. . . .' So . . . Calley and Meadlo got on line and fired directly into the people. There were bursts [of fire] and single shots for two minutes. . . . The people screamed and yelled and fell. I guess they tried to get up, too. They couldn't, that was it. The people were pretty well messed up. Lots of heads were shot off, pieces of heads and pieces of flesh flew off the sides and arms. They were all messed up. Meadlo fired a little bit and then broke down. He was crying. . . . He put his weapon into my hands. I said I wouldn't. 'If they're going to be killed, I'm not going to do it. Let Lieutenant Calley do it,' I told him."

Another witness was Charles Sledge, also a soldier in Calley's platoon. In the first part of his testimony, he told more or less the same story that Conti had told. But then he added that, after the shooting, he had gone with Calley to meet with Staff Sergeant David Mitchell, who was guarding twenty to thirty more villagers near an irrigation ditch. At first, he said, Calley and Mitchell only shoved the people into the ditch with their rifles, but then they started shooting them. They continued to fire into the crowd of people in the ditch until they were interrupted by Hugh Thompson, the helicopter pilot. Next, said Sledge, he and Calley approached a Vietnamese priest. "At least I think he was a priest," Sledge said, "because he was dressed in white robes. Lieutenant Calley started to ask him some questions and the priest, he would fold his hands and bow his head . . . and he kept saying 'no Viet.' Then Lieutenant Calley hit him with the butt of his rifle."

"Where did he hit him?" the prosecutor asked.

"Across the mouth; his mouth was bleeding and then he fell back a little and folded his hands, sort of like pleading. Lieutenant Calley took his rifle and pointblank pulled the trigger right in his face and blew half his head off. . . ." After that, Sledge continued, Calley spotted a small Vietnamese child about two years old. He grabbed the child, threw it into a ditch, and shot it.

Private First Class James Dursi also took the witness stand. Dursi had been guarding a different group of villagers from the ones Meadlo and Conti had been guarding. "Calley came to where I was standing with my people, in front of the ditch," Dursi recalled. "Calley came first, and he was followed by Paul Meadlo. Meadlo was all broke up. He was crying. . . . Lieutenant Calley said, 'Meadlo, we've got another job to do. . . . Kill the people in the ditch. . . .' Then Lieutenant Calley gave the order to shoot . . . and [he] and Meadlo started firing into the ditch."

"Did you fire when Lieutenant Calley ordered you to?"

"No. I just stood there. Meadlo turned to me after a couple of minutes and said, 'Shoot! Why don't you shoot? Why don't you fire?' He was crying and yelling. I said, 'I can't; I won't.' And the people were screaming and crying and yelling. . . ."

After this testimony, the prosecution rested its case. In all, some thirty-five persons had testified. Throughout the testimony, the defense attorneys had cross-examined these witnesses in at-

Calley walks past a row of television cameras as he leaves the courtroom.

tempts to make their statements less believable. The defense attorneys had suggested that the witnesses had something against Calley, or were protecting themselves or their friends, or were smoking pot and were therefore unable to remember as well as being morally unreliable. The witnesses, however, stuck to their stories. The defense also suggested that helicopter and artillery fire had killed the civilians before the soldiers arrived at My Lai.

PAUL MEADLO TAKES THE STAND

Defense counsel George Latimer then began his defense of Lieutenant Calley, but the prosecution interrupted him not long after he began. Something had happened; the prosecution wanted to tell its story one more time. By now, the bloody story had been told so many times that no one really wanted to hear it again. But one more witness had decided to testify. That witness was Paul Meadlo, and everyone wanted to hear what Meadlo had to say.

Meadlo began by describing how he had been guarding some of the villagers, including a number of women and children. "We suspected them of being Vietcong," he said, "and as far as I'm concerned, they're still Vietcong. Calley said to me, 'You know what to do with them, Meadlo.' I assumed he wanted me to guard them.

That's what I did. But Calley came back later, and said 'How come they're not dead? I want them dead.' Then he backed off twenty or thirty feet and started shooting the people . . . and I helped shoot them."

"How were you feeling at that time?" Daniel asked.

"I was mortally upset; scared . . ."

"Were you crying?"

"I imagine I was."

Meadlo then described how he and Calley had shot another group of civilians in a ditch, as Private First Class James Dursi looked on. There may have been as many as 100 villagers in this group, Meadlo said, and he and Calley killed them all.

When Meadlo had finished, prosecutor Daniel asked Meadlo whether Captain Ernest Medina, Calley's commanding officer, had ordered him to kill. "I took my orders from Lieutenant Calley," Meadlo replied, "but Captain Medina was there before the ditch and I assumed everything was okay, because if it wasn't I assumed he would put a stop to it. And he didn't, so I assumed it was right. With all the bodies lying around, why didn't he put a stop to all the killings?" Paul Meadlo was then excused from the witness stand.

Aubrey Daniel had built quite a case, presenting a chilling, terrifying picture of what had happened at My Lai. Throughout the testimony, Lieutenant Calley had simply watched and listened, displaying little emotion. Aubrey Daniel's case for the U.S. government was over. Soon it would be Calley's turn to testify.

THE CASE FOR CALLEY

Defense attorney Latimer did not set out to show that no war crimes had taken place at My Lai; that would have been simply impossible because the evidence of mass murder was overwhelming. Instead, the main thrust of his defense was to show that the murders had been ordered by Calley's commanding officer, Captain Medina. The defense claimed that Calley was simply carrying out orders he believed were just and legal. In effect, Latimer was saying that Captain Medina, not Calley, should have been on trial for murder. Latimer also argued that, because of his mental state, Calley might not have been responsible for his acts on that day. Three psychiatrists testified that this was a distinct possibility. At this point, Colonel Reid Kennedy sent Calley to the Walter Reed Army Hospital in Washington, D.C., for a complete psychiatric examination. The Army psychiatrists at Walter Reed found Calley to be legally sane, and the defense was allowed to proceed with its case.

Near the end of February 1971, Lieutenant Calley took the stand to testify in his own defense. Calley began by saying that he had never been told that he was expected to decide whether an order was legal or not. On the contrary, he had been instructed that, if he questioned an order, he was supposed to carry it out first and then make his complaint later.

Calley then testified that, on the night before the My Lai mission, Captain Medina had ordered the soldiers to attack and destroy the village. Everyone in My Lai was either a member of the Vietcong or a Vietcong sympathizer, Medina had said, and all other South Vietnamese civilians had left the area. After his platoon had reached the village, Calley continued, he received a radio call from Captain Medina, who wanted to know what was slowing him down. "Waste the Vietnamese and get my people out in the position they are supposed to be," said Medina. At that point, said Calley, he went over to Private Meadlo: "I told him that if he couldn't move all those people, to get rid of them." After that, Calley testified that he had left.

Calley denied that he had shot any of the civilians who had been described in the charges against him. He admitted killing several people that morning, but they were not, he said, the same ones he was charged with having murdered. Calley did not deny that *his men* had shot the civilians, only that Medina had ordered everyone and everything in My Lai destroyed, and, though this order had been carried out to the last detail, Calley himself had not done it.

Calley was staking his own word against the statements of all those who had already testified against him. It was Calley alone against all the rest. He did admit that he struck a Vietnamese man with the butt of his rifle when the man would not answer his questions. But he denied having shot him. At first, he also denied having shot the two-year-old Vietnamese child. Later, however, Calley changed his testimony and admitted killing a small person whom, he claimed, he had not recognized as being a child until after he had pulled the trigger.

Even if the court-martial board did not believe Calley's version of what had happened, Calley still had his other defense: "I was ordered," he said, "to go in there and destroy the enemy. That was my job on that day. That was the mission I was given. I did not sit down and think in terms of men, women, and children. They were all classified the same [as enemy soldiers], and that was the classification that we dealt with. . . . I felt then, and I still do, that I acted as I was directed, and I carried out the orders that I was given, and I do not feel wrong in doing so. . . ."

Prosecutor Daniel cross-examined him at great length and in great detail, but Calley stuck to his story. He testified that he had not even taken part in the incidents described by so many of the men under his command. Then he stepped down from the witness stand, and the defense rested its case.

A FINAL WITNESS IS CALLED

One more witness was still to be called, however. His testimony was requested not by the prosecution or the defense but by the court-martial board. This last witness was Captain Ernest Medina. Captain Medina arrived at Fort Benning with F. Lee Bailey (one of the country's most famous criminal lawyers) representing him. Medina was calm and cooperative on the witness stand, but his testimony certainly did not help Calley's case. Medina testified that, according to his information, no civilians were left in My Lai and that his unit would face strong opposition and fierce fighting when it arrived. But that was about the only thing on which he and Lieutenant Calley seemed to agree.

According to Calley, Medina had said at the briefing that their job would be "to go in rapidly and to neutralize everything; to kill everything." Then, according to Calley, someone asked: "Do you mean women and children, too?" and Medina had replied: "I mean everything." But when Medina was asked in court whether someone had raised that question at the briefing, Medina replied that it *had* been raised, but that he had replied, "No, you do *not* kill women and children. You must use common sense. . . ." Medina then denied every other statement that Calley had attributed to him.

"Did you at any time . . . order or direct Lieutenant Calley to kill or 'waste' any Vietnamese people?" Medina was asked.

"No sir," he replied.

Captain Medina told his side of the story in detail, and both the prosecution and the defense cross-examined him. Medina did admit to killing a Vietnamese woman but claimed he thought she was armed. He stuck to his story and did not become rattled even under the flurry of questions. When the cross-examinations were over, Medina was dismissed, and, for all practical purposes, the court-martial was over. Lieutenant Calley and Captain Medina had told very different stories. There was additional testimony from others

175

that tended to support Medina's version, and further testimony that tended to support Calley's version. The exact truth may, in fact, never be known.

FINAL ARGUMENTS

In his final argument, Aubrey Daniel repeated the highlights of the testimony and reminded the court-martial board of all the many witnesses who had testified against Calley. It had been proven, he said, that Calley *did kill*—and *ordered to be killed*—unarmed Vietnamese men, women, and children who were purely civilians. For having done these things, Calley was guilty of murder. Furthermore, Daniel argued, Lieutenant Calley would be guilty of his actions even if he had been *ordered* to do these things. Any such order would have been completely illegal, and Calley could not have legally carried it out.

George Latimer based his final argument for the defense on the idea that those who had testified against Calley simply had grudges to bear. He said that the court-martial was really to decide who should be "killed" for the crimes committed at My Lai: Calley or Medina. Clearly, argued Latimer, it should be Medina; Calley was just a good officer, carrying out his orders.

THE FINDINGS

The court-martial of Lieutenant William L. Calley came to an end on March 16, 1971, three years to the day after Calley had led his troops into My Lai, three years from the time that the entire village and its inhabitants had been destroyed. Calley's trial, which had lasted four months, was the longest court-martial in American history. The jury of six officers also took a long time to reach a decision. Thirteen days passed before the court-martial board announced its findings: Lieutenant William L. Calley was guilty of the premeditated murder of twenty-two human beings. On the next day, Calley was sentenced to life imprisonment and taken from the courtroom to the stockade at Fort Benning.

THE PUBLIC'S REACTION

The American public reacted strongly to Calley's conviction. A Gallup poll showed that 80 percent of Americans disapproved of the guilty verdict. Although some people felt Calley was innocent of any crime, the vast majority felt that Calley was being used as a scapegoat. Although few people defended Calley's acts and many began to speak out against American conduct in Vietnam, most people believed that Calley alone was not to blame.

Calley's case became a political issue, and President Richard Nixon decided to intervene. On the president's authority, Lieutenant Calley was removed from the stockade and instead simply confined to his apartment on the army base. There, he could live in complete comfort and with a great deal of freedom. His girlfriend and others could visit him, he could eat and drink what he pleased, and he could work (with a professional writer named John Sack) on a book about his experiences, for which he would be paid at least $50,000.

In August 1971, the commander of the Third Army reduced Lieutenant Calley's sentence from life to twenty years, as court-martial rules permitted. Later, military officials reduced the sentence to ten years in prison. Finally, on November 19, 1974, after having spent only three and a half years in custody in his own apartment, William Calley was paroled and set free.

The legal proceedings have now ended in the case of William Calley, and the ordeal has ended for all the others involved in the My Lai massacre. The memory and shame of My Lai, however, will be a part of American history forever.

Testing Your Understanding

1. Who was Lieutenant William Calley? What was his military training and experience before March 1968?

2. What happened on March 16, 1968, at My Lai?

3. What role did Ronald Ridenhour have in the development of the story of the My Lai incident?

4. What charges were brought against Calley? What evidence was introduced against him?

5. What arguments did Calley and his attorney make in his defense?

6. What was Captain Ernest Medina's involvement in My Lai?

7. What was the outcome of Calley's court-martial? What was his original sentence, and how was it eventually shortened?

8. Why did the American public have sympathy for Calley?

9. Assuming that Calley did have orders to kill everyone, including civilians, at My Lai, do you think he should have followed the order? What would you have done in his place? Are there times when a soldier should ignore an order? If so, when?

15
Allan Bakke

BACKGROUND

Throughout our nation's history, there have often been national efforts to achieve the promise of equal opportunity for all Americans. In the years following the Civil War, for instance, Congress passed the Thirteenth, Fourteenth, and Fifteenth Amendments to the Constitution to remedy the harmful effects of slavery and to give the newly freed slaves full rights as citizens. Congress then enacted the Civil Rights Acts of the 1870s, which required states and individuals to treat blacks and whites equally, particularly in public places.

The federal laws have not always worked, however. The U.S. Supreme Court found those early Civil Rights Acts to be unconstitutional. The Court reasoned that the Fourteenth Amendment did not give Congress the power to order states and individuals to treat people equally. Congress could only prevent states from making laws treating people unequally. Later, in 1896 in the case of Plessy v. Ferguson, the Court approved the "separate but equal" doctrine, which allowed states to practice segregation.

In the 1950s, though, the Court began to change its mind about whether laws that separated blacks and whites were constitutional. Court decisions in the early 1950s admitted blacks to previously all-white graduate schools. Then in 1954 in Brown v. Board of Education, the Court declared that segregated schools were inherently unequal and struck down laws providing separate public schools for blacks and whites. Shortly after Brown, the Court also struck down the old color barriers in public places and services, such as restaurants, hotels, and buses.

Following the Supreme Court's lead, the federal government once again wrote laws spelling out the equal rights of all Americans. The Civil Rights Act of 1964 made it illegal for employers to discriminate against a person on the basis of race, color, religion, sex, or national origin. This time, the U.S. Supreme Court upheld the law; the Court reasoned that Congress has the power to regulate anything to do with interstate commerce and that business and employers are "in commerce."

Even with the new Civil Rights Act, blacks and other minorities lagged behind whites in many resources. In 1960, for example, the average black had 2.7 years less schooling than the average white, little improvement over twenty years before. Comparatively few blacks had doctoral degrees or were employed as professionals, such as doctors or lawyers. The average income of white families was far greater than the income of black families. Many people believed these gaps were caused by decades of slavery and discrimination.

To help end inequality in jobs and education, President Lyndon B. Johnson in 1965 issued a series of executive orders calling for employers and universities to create more job opportunities for minorities and women. Termed "affirmative action," this idea was intended to prevent future discrimination against these groups and to help remedy the effects of past discrimination. Critics of affirmative action felt that favoring minorities was "reverse discrimination," especially when whites were passed over for minorities who appeared less qualified.

Do our laws and Constitution allow for preferred treatment for persons from groups harmed by past discrimination? Or should the law be "colorblind"? These are the legal questions Allan Bakke asked the courts after his application to medical school was rejected and minorities with lower grades and test scores were admitted.

THE BAKKE CASE

Allan Bakke was grim when he read the letter from the university early in 1973. The brief message informed him that his application to the medical school at the University of California at Davis had been rejected. It was not the rejection itself that disturbed Bakke so much; ten other medical schools had already turned him down. He was upset about what he felt had been the reason for his rejection— the color of his skin. Bakke believed that he had been refused admittance to the Davis medical school because he was white.

THE SPECIAL ADMISSION PROGRAM AT DAVIS

The 100 openings for freshman medical students at Davis were filled according to an **affirmative action** admissions policy. The goal of the special admission program was to increase the number of medical students—and medical doctors—from minority groups. When medical schools began affirmative action programs in the 1960s, a very small percentage of medical students were minorities. In 1967 only 735 medical students out of a total of nearly 10,000 were blacks, and most of the black students attended just two medical schools. In 1977 little more than 2 percent of the practicing doctors in this country were black.

In the Davis program, 16 of the 100 openings were reserved for students who were members of minority groups: black, Asian, or Hispanic. Applicants with minority group backgrounds were permitted to compete for all 100 vacancies, but white students, no matter what their academic qualifications, could compete for only 84 slots—the ones not assigned to minority students. The result was that among the students admitted in 1973 were several minority group members with lower academic test scores than Allan Bakke, whose score was in the top 10 percent of those who had taken the medical school admission tests.

After he was turned down, Bakke wrote a letter to the University of California criticizing its admissions policies. He applied again for admission to Davis in the summer of 1973, and he was rejected again. This time, there was some evidence that his complaints about the treatment he had received previously were taken into account in rejecting him once more. There seemed to be only one way for Bakke to gain admission to medical school. That was to start a lawsuit and try to force Davis to accept him.

ALLAN BAKKE'S LEGAL ARGUMENT

In June 1974, Bakke's lawyer filed suit on his behalf in the Superior Court of Yolo County, California. The suit charged that the university's admissions policy violated Bakke's rights under the California Constitution, under Title VI of the 1964 Civil Rights Act, and under the Fourteenth Amendment to the U.S. Constitution. The Fourteenth Amendment provides that no state shall deny any person the equal protection of the law. Title VI of the Civil Rights Act says that: "No person in the United States shall, on the ground of race, color, or national origin, be excluded from participation in, be denied the benefits of, or be subjected to discrimination under any program or activity receiving federal financial assistance."

In many ways, Allan Paul Bakke seemed an unlikely person to place himself willingly in a position of public attention and controversy. A very quiet and private man, Bakke took elaborate steps to shield himself, his wife, and their two children from any personal publicity during the time his case was being tried. He refused all requests for interviews and for photographs. Pictures that were taken of Bakke frequently showed him shielding his face from the camera with books or newspapers. But Allan Bakke's withdrawn, reserved manner concealed a fierce determination to right the great injustice that he felt had been done him.

Born in Minneapolis, Minnesota, of Norwegian ancestry, Bakke was the son of a mailman and a school teacher. He had become interested in medicine relatively late in life. Bakke had trained as an engineer and had served four years in the Marines, including seven months in Vietnam. He was thirty-two years old when Davis rejected his first application.

Allan Bakke

THE TRIAL COURT'S DECISION

The first judicial decision in the *Bakke* case came shortly after a suit was filed in June. In November 1974, a Yolo County Superior Court judge, F. Leslie Manker, ruled that the Davis admissions program had discriminated against Bakke because of his race and, therefore, was invalid. Manker found that the Davis program violated the U.S. Constitution, the California Constitution, and Title VI of the Civil Rights Act of 1964. The judge declined Bakke's request that he be admitted to Davis, however. His decision was limited to can order that the university decide Bakke's application without taking his race into consideration. Since neither Bakke nor the University of California had received the relief they sought, both parties appealed the court's order. Though the appeal would normally have gone from the trial court to an intermediate level appellate court, the importance of the case caused the California Supreme Court to decide to hear it directly on appeal.

The California Supreme Court is regarded as one of the most able in the state court system, and its decisions are frequently cited by other courts and by legal scholars. Therefore, its decision in the *Bakke* case would be an important one. In September 1976, the court decided unanimously that the Davis **affirmative action** program was unconstitutional because it deprived whites of the equal protection of the law. The court ordered the Davis medical school to admit Bakke in the fall.

THE U.S. SUPREME COURT
AGREES TO REVIEW THE CASE

Many civil rights leaders hoped the *Bakke* case would end there. They were afraid that if an appeal were taken to the U.S. Supreme Court, all affirmative action programs would be declared unconstitutional. If that happened many of the benefits that had been so painfully secured by the civil rights movement would be lost. Nonetheless, the University of California decided to appeal the California Supreme Court ruling. In February 1977, the U.S. Supreme Court agreed to hear the case. The stage was now set for a decision by the nation's supreme judicial authority on what many felt would be the most important civil rights case since the integration decision in *Brown* v. *Board of Education* nearly a quarter of a century earlier.

Unlike people of many other nations, Americans have often turned to their courts rather than their elected leaders in establishing national policy on the great social issues of the day. Certainly, this has been true in the area of civil rights. The Supreme Court's decision in the *Dred Scott* case in 1857 upheld white Southerners' control over runaway slaves, even when they escaped to free states. The *Dred Scott* case caused many abolitionists to feel that there were no legal means of ending slavery and thus hastened the start of the Civil War. *Plessy* v. *Ferguson* (1896) established the "separate but equal" doctrine and served as a means of keeping blacks in a position of inferiority to whites for more than half a century. Then, in 1954, the decision of the Supreme Court in *Brown* v. *Board of Education* reversed *Plessy* v. *Ferguson*.

THE ISSUE OF AFFIRMATIVE ACTION

After the *Brown* case, enormous changes took place in the legal status of minority group members. Both governmental and private programs made massive efforts to raise minority economic and educational levels. Among the most controversial of these programs was affirmative action, which lay at the heart of the Bakke controversy. Affirmative action programs were designed to provide special preference in education and employment opportunities primarily for minorities who had previously been denied these opportunities because of discrimination. This special preference was given in order to increase the number of job and school slots filled by minority group members.

The use of affirmative action raised the question of just how far a society could or should go in making up for the effects of past discrimination. As Americans faced this question, many different answers emerged. Some people felt that race should not be taken into account in any decision involving competition for a job or educational opportunity. They believed that these matters should be decided wholly on merit. According to this view, affirmative action was a device for establishing fixed quotas for members of racial groups. It was actually a form of **reverse discrimination,** by means of which whites would be treated in the same unjust way that minority group members had been treated in the past.

Those who supported affirmative action pointed to a need for some kind of program that gave special preference to minorities in order to overcome the effects of past discrimination. Because mem-

184

bers of minority groups had been denied equal opportunities in the past, they were now *under-represented* in the fields of employment and education. In other words, fewer minority group members had good jobs and were well educated than would be expected from the number of minorities in the population as a whole. In order to make up for this lack, minorities should be entitled to special treatment in employment and education for as long as it was necessary for them to catch up to the white majority population. This policy was justified not only as a compensation for past injustice but also as a means of improving the racial situation in the future. If more representatives of minority groups achieved positions of importance in employment and education, they would provide useful role models for young minority group members. They would also serve to expose both whites and minorities to learning and working situations that could help break down barriers between the races.

Between these two opposing views of affirmative action lay a middle position. Supporters of this position agreed that setting aside a fixed number of places for minorities in education or employment did discriminate against whites. They believed, however, that it was permissible to consider minority-group membership as a positive quality in deciding who would be admitted to a school or hired for a job. This would be similar to giving consideration to the athletic skills of prospective college students or the ability to "get along" of job applicants. Such factors were often taken into account in making choices among applicants. In the same way, minority group membership could be considered a "plus" in an applicant's favor without the necessity of establishing fixed racial quotas.

THE ARGUMENT BEFORE THE COURT

All those who had differing viewpoints on affirmative action eagerly awaited the decision of the U.S. Supreme Court in the case of *Regents of the University of California* v. *Bakke.* The interest and controversy that the case had aroused was indicated by the record number of **amicus curiae** (friend of the court) briefs that had been filed concerning it. These briefs—sixty-one in all—had been submitted to the Court by organizations or persons who were not actually involved in the *Bakke* case but who wanted to express an opinion on it. When the case was argued before the Supreme Court on October 12, 1977, the courtroom was packed. Appearing on behalf of the University of California was Archibald Cox, a former solicitor

185

general of the United States who was famous for having been fired as the Watergate special prosecutor in the "Saturday Night Massacre" carried out by President Richard Nixon in October 1973. Cox began his argument to the Court by saying,

> There is no racially blind method of selection which will enroll today more than a trickle of minority students in the nation's colleges and professions. The suggested alternatives such as helping the "disadvantaged" won't work.

Justice Potter Stewart questioned Cox closely about the matter of quotas:

> Cox: I want to emphasize the designation of sixteen places was not a quota.
> Stewart: It did put a limit on the number of white people didn't it?
> Cox: . . . It was not pointing a finger at a group which had been marked as inferior in any sense; . . . it was undifferentiated and not stigmatizing . . . .

When Cox had finished, it was the turn of Allan Bakke's lawyer, Reynold H. Colvin of San Francisco. Colvin began his argument by pointing out that he was interested in securing admission to medical school for his client, not in writing law review articles. It quickly became clear, however, that the Court wanted him to argue the constitutional issues:

> White: Part of your submission is: even if there are compelling interests, even if there is no alternative, the use of the racial classification is unconstitutional?
> Colvin: We believe it is unconstitutional. We do.
> Burger: Because it is limited rigidly to 16?
> Colvin: No, not because it is limited to 16 but because the concept of race itself as a classification becomes in our history and in our understanding an unjust and improper basis upon which to judge people.

Bakke's attorney further insisted that since Bakke was more qualified than some of the minorities admitted, Bakke himself was entitled to admission. Furthermore, the university was not under

186

any court order to remedy any past discrimination on its part; therefore, its affirmative action plan was not necessary.

THE JUSTICES DELIVER THEIR OPINIONS

It was not until eight and a half months later that the Supreme Court announced its decision in the *Bakke* case. This time the courtroom was half-empty when the chief justice led the other eight members of the Court into the courtroom at 10:01 A.M. on Wednesday, June 28, 1978. As is the practice of the U.S. Supreme Court, no prior announcement was made before a decision on the case was reported. The only clue that this day might be somewhat special was the presence in the audience of the spouses of several of the justices, who usually attended only when an important decision was to be announced. After Justice Stewart reported the Court's decision in a matter involving pension benefits and Chief Justice Warren E. Burger delt with a routine court matter, Case No. 76-811,

The U.S. Supreme Court justices who decided the *Bakke* case. Justice Lewis F. Powell, Jr., *second row, second from the right*, provided the deciding vote on each of the major issues.

187

Regents of the University of California v. *Bakke,* was announced. Justice Lewis F. Powell, Jr., a courtly Virginia lawyer who had been appointed by President Nixon in 1971, gave the opinion of the Court. He began:

> Perhaps no case in my memory had so much media coverage. We speak today with a notable lack of unanimity. I will try to explain how we divided. It may not be self-evident.

Justice Powell then reported that, by a five–to–four vote, the Court had decided that Allan Bakke was entitled to be admitted to the University of California medical school. Powell explained this part of the decision by saying,

> The guarantee of equal protection cannot mean one thing when applied to one individual and something else when applied to a person of another color. If both are not accorded the same protection, then it is not equal.

Interestingly, though Justice Powell's opinion was officially the opinion of the Court, he was the only one of its nine members who reached the conclusion that the "equal protection clause" of the Fourteenth Amendment had been violated by the University of California. Justice Powell did *not* think that Title VI of the Civil Rights Act had been violated because the law was designed to deal with discrimination against minorities, not whites. The other four members of the Court who joined Justice Powell in making up a majority on the question of Bakke's admission—Burger, Stevens, Rehnquist, and Stewart—did not agree that Title VI was solely for the benefit of minority group members. They felt that this statute did apply in the *Bakke* case and that, in Justice John Paul Stevens' words, it "required a colorblind standard on the part of government. . . . As succinctly phrased during the Senate debate, under Title VI it is not permissible to say 'yes' to one person, but to say 'no' to another person, only because of the color of his skin." The Stevens group refused to deal with the question of whether the university's actions had violated the Fourteenth Amendment of the Constitution. The four justices said that they had arrived at a decision based solely on Title VI and that the Court's "settled practice is to avoid the decision of a constitutional issue if a case can be fairly decided on statutory ground."

Despite the justices' disagreements on issues, the decision of the Court was clear. A slim five to four majority had decided that Allan Bakke should be admitted to the University of California medical school.

THE FUTURE OF AFFIRMATIVE ACTION

But the larger question of affirmative action itself remained to be settled. In this part of the complicated split decision, Justice Powell joined the remaining four members of the Court—Brennan, White, Marshall, and Blackmun—in voting to uphold affirmative action. Powell argued that, while rigid numerical quotas based on race alone violated the Constitution, universities did have a legitimate interest in developing a student body made up of a variety of individuals. In achieving this goal, race could be taken into account as a "plus" in admissions decisions when it was considered along with other factors such as geographic diversity, ". . . personal talents, unique work or service experience, leadership potential, maturity, demonstrated compassion, a history of overcoming disadvantage, ability to communicate with the poor, or other qualifications deemed important." According to Powell, affirmative action programs based on this principle were in accordance with the Constitution.

The four members of the Court who agreed with Justice Powell on the constitutionality of affirmative action would have gone much further than he in approving programs that gave special preference to minorities. While Powell felt that the Davis program was unconstitutional, a four-member bloc led by Justice William J. Brennan, Jr., would have upheld the Davis program. These justices believed that "Davis' special admissions program cannot be said to violate the Constitution simply because it has set aside a predetermined number of places for qualified minority applicants rather than using minority status as a positive factor."

Because Justice Powell voted *against* the Brennan position, along with justices Burger, Stevens, Rehnquist, and Stewart, rigid quotas such as those used at Davis were declared illegal. But because Powell voted *with* Brennan, White, Marshall, and Blackmun on the general issue of affirmative action, approval was given to programs that consider membership in a minority group as a "plus" factor. As in the decision to admit Allan Bakke to medical school, the Supreme Court's decision to uphold affirmative action was made by a small majority of five justices who agreed upon the conclusion but differed on the reasons for that conclusion.

Demonstrators near the Supreme Court Building in Washington, D.C., ask the court to overturn the decision of the California Supreme Court

In summary, the decision of the Supreme Court in the *Bakke* case was divided in this way:

	Admission of Bakke	Constitutionality of Quotas	Constitutionality of Affirmative Action
Blackmun	NO	YES	YES
Brennan	NO	YES	YES
Marshall	NO	YES	YES
White	NO	YES	YES
Powell	*YES*	*NO*	*YES*
Burger	YES	NO	•
Rehnquist	YES	NO	•
Stevens	YES	NO	•
Stewart	YES	NO	•
	YES 5	YES 4	YES 5
	NO 4	NO 5	• 4

*Four justices claimed that the question of whether race could ever be considered a factor in admissions was not an issue in the *Bakke* case.

190

Public reaction to the *Bakke* case was swift and, like the decision itself, reflected a result that showed no clear winners or losers among the supporters and opponents of affirmative action. Critics of affirmative action claimed that the Supreme Court was permitting a policy of race consciousness to be pursued indirectly while forbidding it directly. Nevertheless, they were glad to see Allan Bakke admitted to medical school and rigid quotas abolished. Supporters of affirmative action felt that the admission of Bakke and the striking down of quotas indicated a sharp change in the Supreme Court's position on civil rights. These people feared that the *Bakke* decision would limit further gains in the area of civil rights, but they were pleased that the concept of affirmative action had at least been upheld. Most observers agreed that many more decisions would probably have to be made by the Supreme Court before the total meaning of the *Bakke* case would be clear.

And what of Allan Bakke himself? His response to his victory was typical. He smiled slightly on hearing the news and then once again ducked away from reporters. A quiet and private man, Allan Bakke kept his true feelings very much to himself.

Testing Your Understanding

1. Who was Allan Bakke? Why did he bring a lawsuit against the University of California at Davis?

2. Describe the affirmative action admissions program in operation at the medical school at Davis at the time Bakke applied. Why do you think the university established this policy?

3. What arguments did Bakke make against the affirmative action program?

4. How did the California courts decide Bakke's case? Why was the case appealed to the U. S. Supreme Court?

5. Why was the *Bakke* case considered to be such an important civil rights case?

6. What did the majority of the U.S. Supreme Court decide about the affirmative action program at Davis? Did this rule apply to all university affirmative action programs? Explain.

7. Imagine that you are an admissions officer at a medical school with no minority students. What steps could you take to increase the enrollment of minority students without violating the Court's decision in *Bakke*?

8. Should employers and schools seek to increase the number of minority workers and students they have? Is preferred treatment for minorities unfair to people like Allan Bakke? Explain.

Glossary

Affirmative action The requirement that an organization take steps to make up for past discrimination in hiring, promotion, or admittance; for example, by accepting more minorities and women.

Alleged Stated; claimed; argued, but not yet proved.

Amicus curiae (Latin) "Friend of the court." One who is not. a party to a lawsuit, but who gives information to the court on some matter of law. The function of an amicus curiae is to call the court's attention to some matter which might otherwise escape its attention.

Appeal A review by a higher court of the actions of a lower court in order to correct legal mistakes or injustice. Also, to ask for such a review.

Assault An attack or threat of harmful physical contact. Also, to make such an attack.

Capital punishment The death penalty.

Capital offense An offense punishable by death or life imprisonment.

Certiorari (Cert.) (Latin) "To make sure." A request for certiorari is an appeal which the higher court is not required to accept. In other words, if a party files a writ of certiorari with the U.S. Supreme Court, the Court may choose whether to hear the case.

Circuit court

A nineteenth-century term for the federal courts hearing matters involving federal law in the various states. Named originally because federal judges "rode circuit" to serve outlying areas. Subsequently, the circuits were divided into districts. Federal district courts conduct trials; appeals from the district courts go to the federal circuit courts of appeal.

Circumstantial evidence

Evidence that tends to prove a principal fact by proving other events or items that are used to conclude that the principal fact occurred. For example, the fact that a person was seen indoors with wet shoes is "circumstantial evidence" that the person walked in the rain.

Civilian

A person who is not a member of the armed forces.

Clemency

Reducing the punishment of a criminal; mercy.

Closing argument

The statements made by attorneys for each side at the end of a trial, which advise the jury of the issues involved before its deliberation. Closing arguments explain why the jury should decide for one side but are not part of the evidence.

Complaint

A legal paper describing the wrong or harm done to a person by another and requesting specific help from the court.

Commute

To lessen the severity of a sentence.

Conspiracy

Two or more persons planning and taking steps to commit an unlawful act.

Contempt of court

Any act to embarrass, hinder, or obstruct the court in the administration of justice.

Conviction   The finding of guilt as a result of a criminal trial.

Copperhead   A person in the northern states who sympathized with the South during the Civil War.

Court of inquiry   A group of military officers who investigate the facts of an event to determine whether to proceed with a general court-martial. A court of inquiry does not determine guilt or innocence.

Court-martial   A military court used for trying offenses by members of the armed forces. A general court-martial is authorized to try defendants for all military offenses and to give sentences upon conviction. Also, a military trial by court-martial.

Criminal negligence   The causing of injury or death to a person by doing something recklessly or by grossly failing to do something that should have been done.

Cross-examination   The questioning of an opposing witness during a trial or hearing.

Custody   The care and keeping of something or someone, such as a child.

Defendant   In a civil case, the person against whom a claim is made. In a criminal case, the person charged with committing a crime.

Defense   The sum of the facts, law, and arguments presented by the party against whom a legal action, either civil or criminal, is brought.

Deputy   A private citizen who has been legally designated as a temporary law enforcement officer.

Direct evidence   Evidence that does not need other facts to support it; for example, using a live dodo bird to prove that dodo birds are not extinct.

Discrimination
The unequal treatment of a person or persons on a basis other than individual merit. Discrimination can be illegal when based on a person's race, religion, sex, or age.

Dissenting opinion
A judge's formal (written) disagreement with the decision of the majority of the judges on an appeal.

Due process of law
The idea, stated in the Fifth and Fourteenth Amendments, that every person involved in a legal dispute is entitled to a fair hearing or trial. Due process of law protects and enforces individual rights, such as the right to life, liberty, or property, when those rights could be affected by the government's power.

Equal proection of the law
A constitutional guarantee of the Fourteenth Amendment, which protects against unlawful discrimination by the states.

Espionage
The crime of spying or using spies to give information to a foreign country.

Evidence
All types of information, including testimony, documents, and concrete objects, presented at a trial or hearing to prove facts.

Eyewitness
A person who can testify as to what he or she saw, heard, smelled, tasted, or touched.

Federal crime
A crime against the United States.

Felony
A serious crime with a sentence of one year or more.

Freedom of speech
The First Amendment right to say and to hear what you want as long as you do not interfere with others' rights. The constitutionally protected right to the freedoms of speech, of the press, of assembly, and to petition the government are not

196

absolute rights, but each will usually be protected under the First Amendment.

Fugitive

A person who commits a crime and then runs away, often to another state.

Guilt beyond a reasonable doubt

A level of proof required to convict a person of a crime. The jury must be fully convinced that the prosecution has proven each and every element of the crime beyond a reasonable doubt.

Guilty

Responsible for committing a crime; convicted of committing a crime.

Immunity

The freedom from being brought to trial given in exchange for information or cooperation.

Informant

A person who provides information to police about a suspect or about criminal activity.

In forma pauperis

(Latin) "As a pauper" (a very poor person). The permission to sue in court without paying any court costs.

Intent

A state of mind in which a person knows and desires what will happen as a result of his or her act.

Interrogation

The process by which persons are formally and systematically questioned by police.

Judge advocate

A military legal officer who may act as a judge or lawyer.

Jurisdiction

The power of a court to hear a case. Jurisdiction is determined by factors such as the residencies of the parties, the subject matter involved, and the place where the act in question occurred.

Jury

A group of citizens who determine guilt or innocence in a criminal case and responsibility and damages in a civil suit.

Jury list A list of names from which jury members are drawn.

Larceny Stealing of any kind.

Libelous Published written statements that are false and that injure a person's character or reputation.

Lynch law The taking of the law into one's own hands; punishment, usually by hanging, without a trial.

Magistrate A public official in the justice system who can issue warrants for searches and arrests; for example, a justice of the peace.

Majority opinion The formal (written) reasons and conclusions agreed to by more than half of the judges for a decision on appeal.

Martial law Government by the military. In the United States, martial law may exist only in times of war.

Military commission Appointed civilians and officers in the armed forces who decide as a group whether the person charged with a violation of martial law is guilty or innocent.

Military tribunal A military body with the authority to adjudicate matters; a military court.

Mistrial A trial that has no legal effect because of a major defect in procedure. The defendant may be tried again.

Opening statements (Opening arguments) The statements made by the attorneys for each side at the beginning of a trial to advise the jury of the issues involved and to give a general picture of the facts. Opening statements are not evidence.

Overrule To overturn; for a court of appeals to decide that a previous decision in a different case, by that court or by a lower court, was incorrect. For example, in *Gideon*, the Court overruled its previous decision in *Betts*. After *Gideon*, the *Betts* case could no longer be referred to as a Supreme Court precedent.

Pardon   A president's or governor's power to release a person from punishment for a crime. Also, to make such a release.

Parens patriae   (Latin) "Parent of the country." The doctrine under which the court protects the interests of a juvenile.

Parole   The release of a prisoner before his term has expired on the condition of continued good behavior.

Party   A person or institution who starts a criminal or civil case or a person or institution against whom such a case is brought.

Perjury   The crime of lying in court while under oath.

Plaintiff   The party that institutes a suit in court.

Precedent   An appellate court decision on a question of law that gives direction on how to decide a similar question of law in a later case with similar facts.

Probation   Allowing a person convicted of a criminal offense to stay out of jail under supervised conditions.

Prosecute   To proceed against a suspect by charging him or her with a crime and bringing him or her to trial.

Radical   The tendency to make extreme changes. Also, a person with extreme political, social, or religious views.

Rape   The crime of forcible sexual intercourse with an unwilling partner. Also, to commit such a crime.

199

Reprieve

A temporary suspension of the enforcement of a criminal sentence. Also, to delay such enforcement.

Reverse discrimination

Unequal treatment of a person or persons resulting from favorable treatment of other persons who had been previously discriminated against. Reverse discrimination is often claimed by white males who are treated unfavorably when blacks or women are treated favorably to make up for the effects of past discrimination. (See also *affirmative action*.)

Right to counsel

The right of the accused in a criminal trial to be represented by an attorney.

Saboteur

An enemy agent who in time of war intentionally destroys railroads, bridges, machinery, or buildings.

Sanction

To permit or make valid. Also, to punish.

Search warrant

See *warrant*.

Segregation

The separation of persons based on race.

Sentence

The punishment, such as a fine, time in jail, or death, given to a person found guilty of a criminal charge. Also, to give such punishment.

Stay

To stop or hold off. To stay a judgment is to prevent it from being enforced.

Submission (of evidence)

The offering of evidence to a court so that a judgment can be reached.

Summing up

To explain briefly, at the completion of the trial, the main points made by each side during the trial. Also known as the closing statement. A closing statement is not evidence.

Suspended sentence A sentence whose imposition or execution has been withheld by the court on certain conditions.

Test case A case brought to establish an important legal principle or right.

Testimony The oral evidence given by a competent witness under oath or affirmation.

Treason The act of a United States citizen helping a foreign government to overthrow, make war against, or seriously injure the United States.

Trial by jury A trial in which the jury listens to testimony, considers evidence, and decides the factual disputes.

Try To test in court; to conduct a trial of; to act as a lawyer in a trial.

Verdict The opinion of the jury, or of a judge sitting without a jury, on questions of fact.

Verdict contrary to the evidence An opinion reached by a jury that lacks any reasonable support in the facts of the case. In such a situation, the judge may reverse the jury verdict and the defendant can be retried.

Warrant The written permission, based on probable cause, given by a judge or a magistrate to a police officer, allowing the search of a place or the arrest of a person.

War crime A crime committed during or in connection with war.

Witness A person who gives evidence under oath in a court.

Writ of habeas corpus Habeas corpus means literally "you have the body." A written command given by a judge to a person holding a prisoner that requires that person to bring the prisoner to appear before a judge. It is most often used to release a person from unlawful imprisonment.

201

Index

†